The Encyclopedia of
MODELMAKING
Techniques

The Encyclopedia of
MODELMAKING
Techniques

Christopher Payne

Eagle
Editions

A QUANTUM BOOK

Published by Eagle Editions Ltd
11 Heathfield
Royston
Hertfordshire SG8 5BW

Copyright ©MCMXCVI
Quarto Publishing plc.

This edition printed 2001

ISBN 1-86160-418-1

QUMEMT

This book is produced by
Quantum Publishing
6 Blundell Street
London N7 9BH

Printed in Singapore by
Star Standard Industries Pte Ltd

Contents

Structures

Landscapes

Figures and animals

Vehicles and machinery

Introduction

People have been making and enjoying models for centuries. Miniature replicas exercise a fascination that seems to be part of human nature, as the earliest archeological artifacts show – from the ivory objects of prehistoric times to the figures found in the tombs of the pharaohs that we can still admire in our museums today.

The closer we get to modern times, the more examples there are of fine modelmaking. Model ships carved from bone by French prisoners-of-war in Napoleon's time, at the beginning of the 19th century, are prized and valuable possessions. An impressive representation of the Battle of Waterloo (1815), with thousands of model soldiers and guns demonstrating the action, can be seen in Britain's National Army Museum. It looks like a modern diorama, but was made in the years following the battle.

In the 18th and 19th centuries, shipbuilders realized the practical value of models in showing customers how a design would look. Some of our knowledge of the history of ship construction comes from these models, which were often highly detailed. At a popular level, the "ship in a bottle," made by sailors of old, is one of the best known of all models.

Nearly all of the great technical developments of the industrial age have involved modelmaking, which was sometimes fundamental to the production process. The French inventor Denis Papin (1647–1714), who pioneered the development of the steam engine, made all of his experiments by means of models. And the multitube boiler, which was fundamental to the operation of steam power, was demonstrated in model form by another Frenchman, Marquis de Jouffroy, in 1784, some thirty-five years before George Stephenson built the *Rocket*, the first successful steam locomotive. Models that survive from the early days of the railroads predate photography and show us how the original trains looked. As in shipbuilding, models played an important role in persuading skeptical financiers to invest in the railroads.

Early aviators also did many of their experiments with models. Orville Wright (1871–1948) recounts that he and his brother Wilbur (1867–1912) were inspired to fly by their father's gift of a rubber-powered toy that could hop off the ground. The brothers made larger copies of this, which flew even better. Later, they carried out tests on a model of their first flying machine before undertaking their pioneering flight at Kitty Hawk in 1903.

Even modern computer simulation has not replaced the need for models, which continue to be used in commerce and industry, science and education, military operations, and

Right Large scale contemporary scratch-built figures of a British naval officer (left) and local army and militia regiments in Australia made in about 1820, and now part of a historical display.

Left An example of a late 18th century ship model from the still-surviving Buckler's Hard shipyard, Hampshire, where this type of ship was actually built. New ships were frequently first made in model form – an early example of the practical uses of modelmaking.

transportation. Most new building developments are demonstrated by architectural models as part of the planning procedure. Travel offices often have window displays featuring airliners or cruise ships. Museums display models of historical events or use them for educational purposes. In Normandy, France, for example, the D-Day museum at Arromanches contains a panoramic model of the Allied invasion of Europe on June 6, 1994, showing precisely how the landings looked from the position of the museum on the beach. Many of us are familiar with spaceships, and how they operate, by having seen models of them in museums, or by building replicas from plastic construction kits.

Everyday objects and figures have also been miniaturized over the centuries to serve as toys for children. Dolls, dolls' houses, and model soldiers are classic examples. Kings and generals, including Frederick the Great (1712–86), are said to have learned their first military lessons with the aid of toy soldiers. Toys are often fine models, and they kept abreast of events. Realistic pull-along miniature trains in wood or metal appeared almost as soon as their first full-size counterparts.

Working model steam engines of the 19th century were prone to spill hot water and oil over the nursery floor.

These were the status toys of their day, and they evolved into the train sets and other realistic tinplate toys for which Germany was especially renowned. The Germans were also responsible for the development of the mass-produced cast lead toy. Toy

soldier manufacturers evolved the idea of "constant scale," to boost sales of their product, adopting a common size of 1¼in (30mm), then again 1½in (40mm), and finally 2¼in (54mm).

The 20th century saw the development of the scale models that we know today. Manufacturers discovered that the more realistic their

Left Early hand-made model soldiers depicting a French lancer regiment trumpeter of the Napoleonic era and a Prussian Grenadier of the time of Frederick the Great.

models, the more popular they were. Technological achievements, such as streamlined trains, record-breaking automobiles and airplanes, gave a big boost to model development. Mass production made miniature railroads, aircraft, and ships, as well as soldiers, widely available at affordable prices. Magazines, books, movies, and radio publicized events, and caught the imagination of young people, who began collecting and building models.

Construction kits appeared during the 1930s, and were mainly of cardboard, wood, or metal. The earliest plastic kits were produced in 1938, but they did not take off until the mid-1950s. Over the following years, numerous companies began making a huge and ever-growing selection of plastic kits, from aircraft to windmills. The development of plastic kits meant that anyone, with or without technical skill, could assemble fine-looking models. It opened the modelmaking and collection hobby to millions, and has given delight to model enthusiasts from the early 1960s to the present.

Kits have become ever more sophisticated over the years, and include motorized and radio-

Right This is a city waterfront railway scene. The ship was converted from a plastic sailing vessel kit into an early steamer.

controlled models as well as static replicas. Kit-building is highly educational. You learn far more about the original by making a model than by studying a picture or a computer-generated image. Research, which is an enjoyable activity in itself, helps you to complete your model convincingly and can teach you much historical background.

Along with the models have come a wealth of accessories, tools, materials, and paints to put modelmaking within the reach of all. Most people

get their first taste of modeling from plastic assembly kits, which remove the need to shape parts accurately, leaving you with the pleasant tasks of assembly, detailing, and finishing. But the beauty of modelmaking is that if you prefer, you can make models from the most basic materials – scraps of cardboard, wood, and so on – at virtually no cost, just as the 18th-century modeler would have done.

Whether you want to build a model from a kit or make it partly or entirely from scratch will largely depend upon your own interests, and on the time, space and money you have available for modeling. If you like accurate scale replicas, complete in every detail, you will enjoy building a wood, plastic, metal, or cardboard kit. Depending upon its complexity, it might take minutes or

Left This is a good example of imaginative modeling well beyond the limits of ordinary kit building. The structure is primarily wood and the period is the late 1930s.

Left This scenery is typical of the California foothill country at the base of the Sierra Nevada. Note the careful weathering of the locomotive and cars and the realistic use of scale figures.

months to complete. You might then want to put your model in a setting. This will involve study and choice, and probably some research. You might prefer a working model, but bear in mind that these sometimes need modifications of scale to operate correctly. Large-scale kits are, of course, more expensive and will need substantial space and time to complete. Large-scale subjects, on the other hand, can be represented by selective compression.

Most modelmakers today adopt a flexible approach. They work from kits, raw materials, or scrap items as the occasion demands. This book is designed to help you try all of these approaches and get the most out of your modelmaking, whether you are a beginner or already have some experience. It shows how you can improve, adapt, and individualize kits and models, converting them to your own needs or even transforming them to something quite different. We give you clear information about the steps that are needed to put your model together, and in what order to take them, and offer you hints for improving your construction methods. We examine the materials and processes involved in the construction of different types of models, and show you ways to adapt everyday

materials as well as modifying the basic kits. We give suggestions for designing, painting and finishing, projects to copy or use as inspiration, and examples from the many fascinating areas of modeling.

Step-by-step illustrations and instructions show you what is available, what to look for, and what approach will enable you to get the best out of your chosen subject. Each of the subjects covered can be developed in countless ways according to your own personal inclinations, and we give you the tips to enable you to

set off in the direction you choose. If you are a beginner, you will be able to decide which type of modeling activity to take up; if you are more experienced, you will find solutions to problems, some new methods to try, and other projects and developments to explore. Whatever your level of achievement, it is always a good idea to experiment with more than one type of modeling, if only for variety – and also because you are likely to make some interesting discoveries.

Above This British Great Western Railway locomotive of the 1880s is made entirely from scratch of brass and nickel-silver, with all components either machined, formed, or turned on a lathe.

Design

In an age when the word "design" is all too often associated with making products look attractive to potential consumers, its real significance can be lost. Put simply, design is about finding the best solution for a need, and appearance is only one aspect of it.

Design is an integral part of modelmaking. It seeks solutions to initial problems and to those that form part of the production process. An unsuccessful result can be a useful stimulus to revision of the design, and so the process continues. This does not mean that design can be developed piecemeal as a project develops. The more complete your planning, the quicker and easier the construction is likely to be.

Design is the most important – and some would say the most exciting – element of a modelmaking project. It can make the difference between an indifferent model and a fine one. Whether you are seeking to please, to inspire, to communicate certain ideas, or evoke a particular time or place, you will need design solutions. These are likely to concern space, cost, and skill, and unless you are simply assembling a kit of parts, they will involve varying degrees of challenge.

Objectives, inspiration, and research

Models indicate the passions and interests of the builder. Exactly what inspires each individual is not always easy to define, but something needs to catch your imagination and stimulate the desire to recreate in miniature. Inspiration can arise from research, and a vast amount of material is available on a range of potential modeling subjects. Books and magazines, accurate drawings and paintings, photographs, film, and video, museum exhibits, field trips, and personal recollections can all spark your imagination and provide ideas for design approaches. Do not forget also the inspiration that can come from the work of other modelmakers, especially at exhibitions where you can discuss the models with their builders.

Prototype or freelance?

Some modelmakers like to copy the prototype as precisely as they can, while others prefer to invent a subject – a procedure known as "freelancing." A third and much used option lies midway between the two: modeling something that did not exist, but could easily have done so. This is an especially useful approach for military and railroad modelers, who might represent a specific vehicle or piece of rolling stock, but display it in an imaginary setting.

Left Take reference photographs if you are planning to make a model. These will remind you of exactly where parts go and which parts are needed. You can compare relative positions of bar, supports, and frame details, and by knowing the height of the nearest corner post you can figure out approximate sizes for other items.

This kind of container (above) is used as a storage facility as well as for transporting materials.

The model (below) is totally scratchbuilt, using Plastruct ABS plastic.

Planning

After deciding what to model, and conducting your research, it is advisable to prepare some drawings or sketches. Sometimes a good alternative is to make a rough model. This could be full-size – in the case of a single military figure in a setting, for example – or to a reduced scale for a subject such as a railroad layout. This is a valuable phase, because it gives an idea of how the finished model will look. Changes can then be easily made if necessary. Often a slight departure from the prototype – in the exact grouping of a number of buildings, for example – can improve the appearance of the resulting work. An attractive original does not always make a successful model without the element of artistic licence.

Ease of construction

There is usually more than one way of approaching a problem, and there may not be an ideal method. It is often said that the best way of doing something is the way that works for the particular individual. In the case of large and sophisticated models, it is wise to think in terms of a series of

Left Several buildings with one of the design drawings. At this stage the structures are simply shells of foamboard.

Left Comfortable working conditions are essential for good modelmaking. Work at a height suitable for the bench, which enables you to rest your forearms conveniently.

Above Continue to check your plans as the work progresses. Here, buildings are posed together at an early stage to check that they fit together.

Left Careful planning has permitted an evocative scene in a relatively confined space.

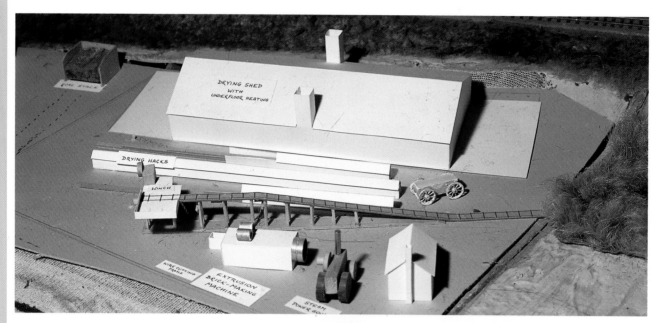

sub-assemblies, and to give clear consideration to how they will fit together. The idea of sub-assemblies is also useful when planning the painting of a model; even if the work is made in one piece, there are aspects of painting that are best tackled during the construction rather than at the end. This needs forethought, especially if the various stages are to be integrated as a convenient uninterrupted sequence.

Operation

Models that incorporate movement, such as railroad locomotives, need consideration of how they are to be powered, where the motor should go, and how access can be provided for its maintenance. You must consider how the movement is to be controlled, which means making allowance for wiring runs, providing control panels, and including rodding and levers for mechanisms.

Display, transportation, and lighting

When the model is complete, where will it be sited? How will it be viewed, and by whom? Dust is the ever-present enemy of the model: at

Left The importance of a flat working surface and good lighting can be seen in this shot where details are added to the interior of a model railroad car.

best, it can make it look dowdy, and at worst, it can prevent a working model from operating. A single military figure might be displayed and stored under a glass or transparent plastic dome. Larger models, such as dioramas and railroad layouts, will need some other provision. Traditionally railroads are displayed at fairly low levels, but this means that the viewer sees a lot of roofs. Far more acceptable is a minimum track

height of 4ft (1.25m) for public display, and 5ft (1.5m) or more for home use. The height suggested for exhibits is a compromise: the ideal for most adult viewers is around natural eye level, but consideration must be given to children and wheelchair users.

Exhibiting models publicly can be challenging and rewarding. If you are going to do this, you must consider how to transport your models easily and safely. The obvious answer is a protective carrying case, and you need to allow for its provision and fixing at the design stage. Here again, a compromise may be necessary in order to achieve a satisfactory degree of protection without adding excessive weight.

There is no point in putting hours of work into a model only to display it in such gloomy conditions that all of its finer points go unnoticed. Adequate lighting is essential for both home and exhibition display, and you cannot rely on that provided in the environment. Individual models, dioramas, or even large areas of railroad need their own lighting. Think of the model on display as a small piece of theater and light it accordingly.

Some people would advise complex systems that use sophisticated bulbs, fittings, dimmers, and colored filters. This is fine, but not essential. Simple tungsten bulbs carefully positioned behind the proscenium arch of a staged presentation, for example can be highly effective. You will need to take precautions against excessive heat, and also remember to paint the model under the light you will be using for display.

Above The juxtaposition of railroad track, warehouse, quayside, water, and boat provide an interesting three-dimensional composition.

Left The design of model railroad layouts calls for particular skills. This is especially so when space is limited, and you need to bring together several elements and working components. This view of a layout shows a quayside railroad track that permits the unloading of tipper trucks into a waiting boat.

Tools

Whatever your level of skill or the kind of models you want to make, you will need certain basic tools. Although you can, of course, purchase a superb and extensive toolkit, a variety of power tools, and even a luxury workbench, that is fortunately not necessary. Many of the tools used for the projects in this book can be found in most households for the purpose of carrying out everyday domestic repairs. Additional tools are readily available from hardware, modelmaking, art supply stores, or building supply centers.

The basic toolkit lists all the tools you need to assemble and convert plastic construction kits, or build models from materials such as cardboard and wood. This will be sufficient for most of your modeling work – possibly all of it – and you can store the tools in a cardboard box. As you gain experience, you may discover that there are other specific tools that would be helpful for the particular area in which you enjoy working.

Power tools, such as the jigsaw, or sabre saw, speed up certain types of work, but are not essential. The single more expensive tool that you should consider is the airbrush, because it can help you achieve paint effects that are not possible with a regular paintbrush. This is especially valuable for simulating the finish on the metal of vehicles and for applying a well-blended and varied tone to certain scenic work. It also enables you to create the effects of aging, wear, and weathering, although here dry-brushing by hand can also be excellent.

Marking and setting out

To produce a satisfactory model, the components must fit accurately together, which means that they must be correctly shaped. This is achieved by precise marking, with the aid of a ruler calibrated in suitable measurements, an H or 2H pencil to mark points and draw lines, and a try square to establish and check right angles. Although a triangle is fine for producing right angles on drawings, the try square (sometimes known as an engineer's square) is especially good for setting out corners on styrene sheet, mat board, or stripwood. One with a blade of about 4in (100mm) should suit most needs.

Cutting, shaping, and drilling

Much of the cutting and shaping involved in modelmaking is done with knives. Modeler's knives are available from a number of companies, but a popular choice is the kind consisting of interchangeable handles and blades, such as the X-Acto knife. Most of the blades are made specifically for carving and other art and craft tasks, and you can obtain a variety of shapes to suit different jobs. The long, finely pointed, scalpel-like blades are extremely sharp and will permit accurate and delicate cuts. They can be sharpened with a whetstone, but are easily replaced. Fit a wedge-shaped blade for sturdier cutting jobs, or use a heavy-duty craft knife, such as the kind with snap-off blades. This provides a long blade that has been scored along one side. As the cutting edge becomes dull, you can break off that section and advance a new section of blade in the knife handle.

Cutting often needs to be done in straight lines, and for this a metal straight-edge is essential. You can use the blade of your try square when appropriate, but a metal ruler is generally the most suitable tool. It is a good idea to have separate rulers for measuring and cutting. A plastic ruler is fine for measuring, but do not use it for cutting, because it will be damaged by your blade.

The other cutting tools you will use are saws. The miniature saw known as a razor saw is best for small-scale and delicate work. Coping saws are suitable for cutting plywood, and a tenon saw for materials such as chipboard used for bases. You can use an electric saw instead – the jigsaw, or saber saw, is the most useful.

Pliers are needed for shaping metal, such as wire. The round-nosed model is usually best, because it does not mark the piece. Use side cutters to make cuts, and needle files to smooth them. Needle files will find even greater use on materials such as styrene sheet and tube. The inexpensive kind are suitable.

Similar in application and effectiveness to needle files are various abrasive products. Emery boards are very useful for rubbing down rough edges on plastic models, and wet/dry paper is good for achieving a smooth finish on stripwood and styrene. A very fine "finishing" paper produces an excellent surface on plywood prior to painting for display purposes. You can polish out scratches that occur on clear plastic – when making windows, for example – with the aid of a mild

Left A "dry run" is always useful before kit assembly. Here the main parts of an aircraft kit are held together temporarily with masking tape to check the assembly sequence.

abrasive, such as toothpaste.

The tools needed for making holes will depend upon the size of the holes and the material being worked. A regular household power drill can be used for plywood, and there are miniature electric drills that take a similar range of tools for more delicate work, but these are not essential. A miniature screwdriver is more than adequate for making small-diameter holes in styrene sheet and plastic kit components. This can come from a set of screwdrivers, which will be useful for making different-sized holes and for helping to insert filler into a small gap, as well as for their intended function. A hand-held chuck, along with a set of pin drills, is also useful. The drilling is done by rotating the chuck between thumb and forefinger – especially practical when making tiny holes for attaching wire handrails, for example. An ordinary bradawl can also be excellent for many tasks.

For detail work, such as carving brick or stone on the modeling clay-covered shells of buildings, you will need a scriber. And for simulating planking on a sheet of styrene, you must fit a hook blade to your knife. Do not be tempted to use another tool for this; only the hook blade will cut a clean groove and remove the

surplus material at the same time. Miniature sculpting tools for shaping items built in two-part epoxy putty are carried by hobby and art supply stores, or you can use dental probes.

Assembling and joining

The standard method of joining pieces of plywood is to pin and glue them together with small pins and white glue. This means that you need a small hammer in your toolkit. An alternative is to use a heavy-duty staple gun capable of firing ⁹⁄₁₆in (14mm) staples into wood. This method can be effective even for relatively large baseboards, and is easier than aligning the work accurately while simultaneously holding the pin and wielding the hammer.

A regular office stapler and staple pliers are also useful for tacking together cardboard strips when building the frame for a scenic shell, although this can be done with a hot glue gun.

Sometimes it is necessary to hold two components in juxtaposition while they are being joined. You can keep them together by attaching them temporarily to a piece of cork with dressmaking pins. For simple clamping – while glue sets, for example – use clothespins or small crocodile clips.

Optional additional items include a small bench vise that clamps to the edge of a table or workbench to hold items steady, leaving both hands free. D-clamps (also known as G-clamps), which come in a range of sizes, hold a section, such as an aircraft wing, to the surface while you work on it, or keep parts together while glue dries. There is also a device specifically for modelmakers, known as a handy clamp, which consists of a stand with an adjustable selection of rods, clamps, and spring clamps, and usually a magnifying glass. You can set the clamps at varying angles to hold small components for painting and drilling, setting the magnifying glass over them for a close view of intricate work.

Finishing

Finishes usually consist of paint and varnish. This can be applied by hand or airbrush. For hand-brushing, use good-quality artist's brushes in a variety of sizes and shapes. Sable brushes are the best choice, and you will need flat and round ones.

The airbrush, which comes with a related air supply, works on the same principle as the atomizer, applying paint by means of a controlled spray. It is a relatively expensive item and needs practice to use efficiently. Once you have become familiar with it, however, you will appreciate its usefulness.

The choice of airbrush should be made after some research, preferably with the advice of a good hobby or art store person to whom you have explained your intended use. This is important, because some airbrushes that are good for art and graphics are unsuitable for models, mainly because they cannot spray the heavy consistencies of paint often needed.

The airbrush itself is not the only choice to make, because in order to work it needs a suitable propellant. There are three possible sources: pressurized cans, an inflated automobile tire tube, and a compressor. Cans are convenient and relatively inexpensive, but they are quickly emptied. The tire tube, with suitable connectors, is cumbersome and needs to be regularly reinflated. A compressor is, therefore, the best long-term choice. However, you might

like to begin by trying a simple spray-gun airbrush with canned air to get the feel of this equipment.

Paint-mixing palettes are unnecessary – it is easier to use plastic yogurt pots or the lids of jars and bottles that can be thrown away after use. You will need a trowel-shaped palette knife to apply earth mixes and some varieties of scenic dressing. And a coffee strainer is useful for shaking materials onto glued surfaces.

Specialized tools

The tools listed will equip you well for most general modeling work. If you develop an interest in metal models, or railroad wiring and track, you will also find a small soldering iron essential, and if you do a lot of modeling with metal kits you might want to acquire a miniature power drill that also takes polishers, cutters, and reamers. For more complex pro-

cedures that begin to enter the realms of model engineering, sophisticated carpentry and power tools, lathes, and cutters become necessary, particularly in model railroad work, for example. For those beginning to venture into such areas, the model engineering magazines are useful sources of information concerning specialized equipment and suppliers.

Your work surface

You must have a cutting board to protect your work surface. You can use a piece of masonite or thick, close-grained plywood, but these will become scored and pitted, and must be discarded when they become too uneven or they will affect the accuracy of your work. The best choice, therefore, is a self-healing rubber cutting mat.

Safety

Care in the use of tools cannot be

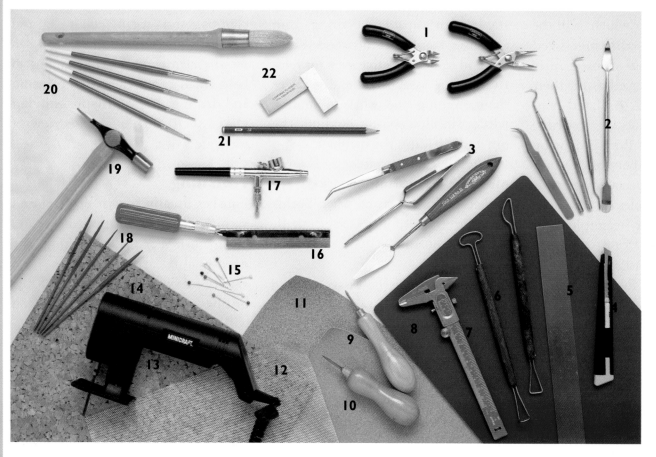

Left 1 Round nose pliers and side cutters; 2 Dental probes; 3 Palette knife and tweezers; 4 Craft knife; 5 Metal ruler; 6 Sculpting tools; 7 Caliper; 8 Cutting mat; 9 Fine bradawl; 10 Pin chuck; 11 Sandpaper (medium and fine grades); 12 Fine mesh gauze; 13 Small jigsaw; 14 Cork tile; 15 Dressmaking pins; 16 Razor saw; 17 Airbrush; 18 Needle files; 19 Hammer; 20 Assorted brushes; 21 Pencil; 22 Try square.

overemphasized. Read and heed the instructions before you begin work, and do not be tempted to skip any precautions however mundane or irritating they seem. Just as you automatically take precautions in the kitchen – another potentially dangerous but welcoming place – make safety second nature in your modeling area, for yourself and others.

Above Before you begin, check that all tools and materials are to hand. Here are the tools needed for plastic kit assembly.

Basic toolkit

- H or 2H pencil and eraser
- Ruler for measuring
- Metal ruler for cutting straight lines
- Try square
- Knife with interchangeable blades, including finely pointed scalpel-type and hook blades
- Heavy-duty craft knife
- Razor saw, coping saw and tenon saw
- Round-nosed pliers
- Side cutters
- Needle file
- Emery board
- Wet/dry paper
- Very fine-grade sandpaper
- Set of screwdrivers, including miniature size
- Bradawl
- Pointed tweezers
- Scriber
- White glue
- Dressmaking pins
- Small hammer or heavy-duty staple gun
- Stapler/staple pliers
- Clothespins or crocodile clips
- Artist's brushes or airbrush
- Self-healing rubber cutting mat

Optional additions

- Pin drill and vise with set of small drills
- Small bench vise
- D-clamp/G-clamp
- Handy clamp
- Small soldering iron
- Power tools, such as drill, jigsaw, or minidrill with a range of drills

Tool safety

- Use tools for the intended purpose and follow the manufacturer's instructions.
- Do not work in a crowded environment.
- Never leave tools rolling around on a work surface where they may fall off and be trodden on. When you have finished with a tool, replace it in the toolbox immediately.
- Remember that a child's eye level can be close to your working height. Do not allow children to play in the area while you are using tools.
- Cut away from the body; keep your fingers behind the direction of the cut.
- Keep your hands well clear of any area being drilled.
- Do not force a knife through thin plastic that will not cut

immediately; you may shatter the blade and send pieces flying. Use the razor saw to do most of the cutting and only complete it with the knife.
- Wear protective glasses when cutting and shaping, especially with power tools. Wear a mask in the presence of fumes and sprays.
- Do not wear loose clothing or jewelry, and tie back hair that might get caught.
- At the end of a modeling session, account for all of your tools and make sure they are in the box.
- Keep an old coffee can with a slot in the lid for any discarded blades – those who handle the trash may be cut by loose blades, even wrapped.
- Use your tools with care and common sense at all times. Think "safety"!

Materials

If you work from plastic, metal, or wood construction kits, you will be supplied with all of the key materials. Sometimes a kit contains additional items needed for completion, such as thread for rigging, or lettering for a model bus. Some aircraft kits consist mainly of molded plastic parts but include etched metal pieces for aerials, footholds, cockpit fittings, and so on. There are exceptions, however. Locomotive or rolling stock kits can omit wheels or couplers, for example, on the grounds that the modeler will want to choose a pattern from those available as accessory parts. Some kits can be motorized but no motor is supplied. In all of these cases, the omissions and options are usually clearly marked on the box or instruction sheet. So when you work from a kit, check the instruction diagrams and the components to make sure that everything you need to make the model is included. Find out whether you need to obtain additional material, and read through all of the instructions before you begin work. You do not want to discover, after construction is well advanced, that you needed to add ballast weights that were not provided – and that it is now too late to fit them to your assembly.

Recycled materials

Keep all of the pieces that are left over when a construction kit is built. Often there are spare items, or parts provided on the mold that are not needed. There are remnants of plastic, wood, or metal, as well as optional markings. These can become useful material for future projects. Store them in a "spares box" made from an old cardboard box, kit container, or nail and screw box with drawers. Any modeler of some years standing has such a box, and it can become your most valuable source of materials. Get into the habit of hoarding all kinds of scrap items and trifles as almost any little oddment will come in handy in modeling.

The materials you collect will vary to some extent with the sort of modeling you do. You can, for example, make miniature buildings and other structures from cardboard salvaged from cereal packaging or the board at the back of some notebooks and sketchpads. Store this cardboard in varying thicknesses in a large shallow box. The same applies to wood. Keep any oddments you find, especially thin pieces. The flimsy plywood sometimes used for vegetable and fruit containers makes good material for small-scale modeling. Leave some pieces outside for a week or two and they will weather, dry out, and separate into layers, making them ideal for fine planking on small models or for shingles on rooftops.

Apart from the sheets and strips of woods of various thicknesses sold in model stores, there are sometimes remnant packs that are worth having. Hardware stores and building supply centers may have an inexpensive collection of leftover lengths, including plywood, chipboard, and masonite. These are good for diorama bases, but pieces can often be used in model construction.

If you make scenic dioramas or model railroad layouts, you can cut and carve polystyrene (Styrofoam) packaging, old plastic, or foam sheet to make terrain, and use household plaster for additional features. Keep used foil containers for mixing paints and holding scenic materials while you work. Cut them up to simulate sheet metal, or score the bases with a ballpoint pen to portray corrugated iron.

Railroad and diorama modelers can also collect items such as old deodorant containers and shampoo dispensers to turn into oil tanks, silo towers, or truck bodies. Aircraft modelers can store up transparent packaging from toothbrushes, packs of screws, or tools to serve as radomes, nacelles, turrets, fairings, and other components.

There are so many suitable scrap materials available that model-making need not be an expensive occupation. But there are also materials that you will need and want to buy from model stores and other sources. They include mat board, styrene sheet, plywood, stripwood, foamboard, and expanded polystyrene. It is also essential to have the correct glue for your chosen material.

Mat board

Mat board has a creamy-colored core, is faced on one side in white, and has a decorated surface on the other. This surface comes in a range of colors, because the purpose of mat board is to frame and display a picture. You can buy it in sheets from art supply stores, but it is worth asking picture framers if they have any remnants. These are usually small rectangular pieces with the edges cut on a 45° bevel. They are mostly useful for

Above 1 Two part epoxy putty; **2** Talcum powder; **3** Styrene strip and tube; **4** Enamel or acrylic paints; **5** Masking tape and electrical insulation tape; **6** Spray adhesive; **7** Two part epoxy glue; **8** Foamboard, expanded polystyrene and clear plastic sheet; **9** Commercial fittings, kit parts; **10** Wire; **11** Twigs; **12** Plywood; **13** Foliage fiber, ground foam and scenic dressing; **14** Cyanoacrylate glue (Superglue); **15** Chipboard; **16** Spackle compound; **17** Pins; **18** Crystals to stimulate water; **19** Stripwood; **20** Modeling clay.

buildings, and almost any color will do, because it is likely to be hidden under the appropriate finishes. In fact, the white face will normally be the outer one, because it will show the necessary marking clearly.

Mat board of 1/16in (1.5mm) thick is particularly suitable for the basic shells of smaller-scale buildings (1:76, 1:87, and less), where it gives adequate recess depth for door and window frames. In larger scales, its use is limited by the need to provide a lot of internal bracing, and by its relative incompatibility with wet materials, such as modeling clays and fillers, applied as surface finishes. Cardboard naturally absorbs moisture, and will deform. This can be prevented by protecting the board with polyurethane varnish, but except for modeling wooden-clad buildings in the larger scales, it is preferable to use a thicker material for the shell.

The advantages of mat board are that it is readily available, inexpensive, clean to work with, and easy to cut with a knife.

Styrene sheet

The plastic used by modelers is styrene sheet – sometimes known as plastic card. Sold under various brand names, it looks like thin postcard, and comes in several colors, including black, white, gray, red, and yellow. There are thicknesses from 10 thousandths of an inch (0.25mm), rising in 10 thou increments to about 80 thou (2mm). Styrene sheet is clean to work, easy to cut, sand, and file, and takes a variety of paint finishes. It is especially useful for representing painted metal, and enables effective construction of locomotives, machinery, and road vehicles in place of metalworking.

There are also packs of styrene strip in all thicknesses for making items such as small-scale window frames and ladders, and packs of rods for drainpipes, aerials, exhaust tubes, and so on.

Styrene sheet should not be confused with the kind of plastics used for rainwater and plumbing products. These are a harder form of plastic, and while they can sometimes be useful, specialist glues are needed to bond them to styrene and other plastics. Styrene, on the other hand, is easy to weld using a suitable solvent.

Styrene is good for making the building shells in the smaller scales, and especially for the portrayal of painted wooden buildings. For a clapboard building, for example, you can simply cover the basic shell with overlapping strips of styrene. It is also useful if you want to apply simulated brickwork, or adapt a building from a plastic kit.

A number of manufacturers produce embossed styrene sheet in a number of scales. The many varieties of finish include brick, stone, corrugated iron, clapboarding, and metal; there is also tile and slate for roofs. Complete models can be built from these materials. The sheets are generally thick enough to be self-supporting when utilized for small structures. For larger ones – or if you use the similar but thinner vacuum-formed sheet – you should apply the material to a suitable shell. This could be made of styrene for easy bonding, but other materials could be used provided you choose a suitable glue.

Styrene is available from model-making stores and is generally more expensive than mat board. Cut it with a sharp blade, or apply the scribe and snap method for thicker sheets. Remember that larger buildings will need some internal support.

Plywood

Plywood is readily available and can be very strong when properly utilized. It bends easily in one plane, but when formed into structures with right angles so that one piece braces another, it becomes sturdy. Use it to form baseboards for small model railroad layouts and dioramas.

It is also suitable for making the shells of buildings, and given the amounts of material needed even in scales such as 1:48, 1:43, and 1:35, plywood will be inexpensive: an 8ft x 4ft (2.5m x 1.2m) sheet will go a very long way, and you can also make use of pieces remaining from building work or home maintenance. Since it only serves as a basic shell, a thickness of around ¼in (6mm) is ideal, and the quality is unimportant, except that the cheaper grades are more likely to splinter when cut, so extra care is needed. Some modelers prefer a thinner plywood of around ³⁄₁₆in (4mm), and for really large-scale work (1:24, for example), ⅜in (9mm) and ½in (12mm) ply would be suitable.

Plywood is fairly easy to cut with simple woodworking tools. You can cut out basic shapes, such as the side of a building, with a tenon saw, and use a coping saw for door and window openings. It is not necessary to drill a hole at the site of a window to permit the unclamped blade of the coping saw to be threaded through, because subsequent finishing of the shell can cover any cut lines from the edge. You should, however, make sure that there is only one cut line for each aperture and that there is no risk of weakening the overall structure of the piece. A power jigsaw fitted with a fine-toothed blade for a smooth cut can be used instead of the coping saw, and will reduce the time

Below Different sizes of plywood in soft and hard woods are carried by leading model stores.

needed for sanding. Bandsaws, and shaper, scroll, and electric fretsaws could also be used.

Plywood shells can be quickly assembled with butt joints by pinning and gluing with white glue woodworking adhesive. Hammer nails of around ¾–1in (20–25mm) length into the joints to keep the pieces correctly aligned while the glue sets. Alternatively, you can secure the parts with a heavy-duty stapler of the kind used for upholstery work.

Plywood shells are strong and cheap to produce, but heavy. For a static model, a single structure, or a ruined building this may be unimportant, but for a diorama or railroad layout that needs to be transported for display, it could be a major drawback.

Foamboard

Foamboard (also known as foamcore) has all the advantages of plywood, styrene, and mat board, except that it costs slightly more. This is outweighed by its qualities. The ¹³⁄₆₄in (5mm) and ¼in (6mm) thicknesses can be made into robust but light structures. Joining is done with white glue on butt joints, using ordinary dressmaking pins to hold the pieces together whilst the adhesive sets – around 5 to 10 minutes.

Marking in pencil is straightforward on the white cardboard surface, and cutting is easily and cleanly achieved using a sharp blade with a long, straight cutting edge. Openings in the shell have a good depth that can represent a considerable thickness of wall, and the slightly giving nature of the foamcore enables you to temporarily force fit doors and windows within this. Warping is no danger provided you coat the exterior

and the interior surfaces of the shell with a dilute white glue solution, and you can then apply surface finishes in wet modeling clay or filler.

These thicknesses are especially suitable for larger scales: 1:48, 1:43, and 1:35. An ⅛in (3mm) thickness would be useful for details such as protruding brickwork or piers, and might be satisfactory for some smaller-scale work, and ⅜in (10mm) thick foamboard could be used in 1:24 scale.

Stripwood

Nothing represents sawn wood on a model as well as wood itself. A good source with which to portray frames and planks is stripwood. This is sold specifically for modelmaking in various sections, and in different woods. Limewood, carried by stores that specialize in model boats, is particularly good, but balsa, though widely available and fine for flying model aircraft, is not always satisfactory for making and detailing structures. You will need to check the supplies in your local area and choose accordingly.

Stripwood is easy to mark, cut, sand, and work. It also bonds readily with a variety of glues, and provided you keep glue away from the surface, it is simple to paint or stain. Staining is especially useful to convey the weathering of unpainted wood over time.

Expanded polystyrene

Expanded polystyrene is most often found in packaging (around television and audio equipment, for example), or in the form of ceiling tiles. The packaging often has the advantage of being several inches thick. Similar material is available in

Above Plywood and plastic strips in various thicknesses are always useful. Keep small remnants and collect any pieces that others discard!

fairly thick sheets and blocks from building supply companies. Take care to use only nonflammable types of expanded polystyrene.

Expanded polystyrene is especially useful for creating land forms on a large or small scale. The results can be quickly seen, and will be lightweight yet solid enough to provide a firm siting for items such as trees. Finishing will be needed in the form of suitable earth mixes and scenic dressings.

There are two main limitations to

the use of expanded polystyrene. First, it is not suitable for structural use, and second, you must choose your glue with care, because some adhesives dissolve it. The most acceptable are white glue and hot-melt adhesive from a glue gun.

Adhesives

There are dozens of different adhesives in hardware stores, houseware counters, stationery, and hobby stores, and this can seem very confusing to the aspiring modelmaker. In this book, we have used a limited number that fulfill most needs. In the case of these and all glues, it is essential to observe the manufacturer's advice on use and safety.

Styrene solvent sticks styrene to itself and to other materials, such as paper and cardboard. It is preferable to the traditional, cement-type glues made for plastics, because it has a watery consistency, does not string, and can be applied very precisely with a fine brush. It will enter the space between pieces to be joined by capillary attraction and form a neat, strong bond.

Cyanoacrylate glue (also known as Superglue) is good for bonding different materials to each other — metal to styrene, for example. It is most suitable for small joints, applied with a pin. It can also be useful for assembling structures made from stripwood, because it dries almost instantly.

Two-part epoxy glues come in separate tubes: an adhesive and a hardener. When mixed, they form exceptionally strong bonds. They are especially effective for fixing white-metal components to styrene. Some varieties set in minutes and others take several hours. It is advisable to allow 24 hours before carrying out additional work on either type. You can then trim the glue back with a sharp knife. It is possible to mix epoxy glues with talcum powder to form a dense gap filler that can be very finely carved.

White glue (polyvinyl acetate) is useful for basic carpentry and will often be in the home already for domestic repairs. Often used in association with pins to hold components together while the glue sets, it can create sturdy, durable joints. It is the adhesive to choose for attaching pieces of foamboard.

Hot glue guns offer the advantage of virtually instantaneous adhesion. They are especially useful in bonding expanded polystyrene to itself or to other materials.

Plastic wood

Plastic wood is available in tubes and sets to a wood-like texture, after which it can be filed and sanded like wood. As a filler for wood modeling it is invaluable, although it may need an extra undercoat before final painting to prevent the plastic wood area showing through.

Paints

For general modelmaking work, three paints serve most needs: enamels and acrylics (sold at hobby stores specifically for models), and

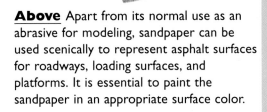

standard household latex paint. The enamels and acrylics are produced by various companies, often in a range of colors intended for specialist use – military and railroad, for example. Latex paint is good for large areas of scenery and for painting the edges and frames of bases, cases, and other aspects of presentation. Latex colors blend easily, the paint dries quickly, and the brushes used can be washed in water. For certain applications, such as painting figures, liquid acrylics and inks suitable for airbrushing are useful.

Acrylics dry speedily, and this makes them unsuitable for the technique of dry brushing – the application by brush of paint that is nearly dry. This lightly covers a base coat with a paler version of the same color (or sometimes white) to introduce a faded, weathered look. It also brings out any surface detail that is in relief. Because acrylic hardens almost instantly on the brush, it will splatter your work with specks of dried paint. Use enamel paint to ensure a subtle coat that adheres to the surface.

Embossed boards and printed papers

Useful for buildings, model railroads, and dioramas – as an alternative to embossed styrene sheet – is thin embossed printed cardboard, portraying bricks, stonework, paving, cobbles, asphalt, planking, and roof materials. Road surfaces, such as asphalt, are available in rolls. As an alternative to commercially available surfaces, you can also use coarse or fine sandpaper, depending on the scale, painted in an appropriate surface color.

Also widely used are printed papers simulating every sort of finish, including brickwork, tiles, slates, stone – even cutout doors and windows. There are wallpapers for interiors that come in the popular miniature rail scales, or in larger scale from dolls' house accessory manufacturers.

<u>Above</u> Apart from its normal use as an abrasive for modeling, sandpaper can be used scenically to represent asphalt surfaces for roadways, loading surfaces, and platforms. It is essential to paint the sandpaper in an appropriate surface color.

Some items for the spares box

- Old ballpoint pens and refills
- Pieces of stiff wire in varying diameters
- Scraps of wood
- Staples
- Paper clips
- Bits of metal
- Discarded nuts and bolts
- Matchsticks
- Self-adhesive address labels
- Spare pieces from kits, including decals
- Anything of an interesting or useful shape

Scales

A key consideration in all aspects of modelmaking is scale. A model is by definition a replica, and it is usually smaller than the original. Instructional models may be enlarged, but most items constructed by the average modeler are miniaturized objects.

In order to make an accurate replica, you need to know exactly how much to reduce the dimensions all the way around, so as to retain the precise proportions of the original. If you do not, your model will be at best inaccurate, and at worst a caricature of the original. Accuracy of scale has obviously concerned modelmakers from the earliest times, since the models found in the tombs of the Pharaohs appear to be finely proportioned replicas. Other historic models, such as the beautiful bone warships made by prisoners of the Napoleonic wars at the beginning of the 19th century, are precisely observed replicas.

A model can be made to any scale. Industrial models of a new aircraft, for example, might be constructed to a half of the plane's proposed size for testing in a wind-tunnel. The dimensions of the full-sized aircraft are simply halved to make a replica. From this we can see that it is possible to reduce the full dimensions by any required factor to come up with a model of convenient size. The factor by which it is reduced is called the scale.

As an example, take a familiar scale for model aircraft: 1:72. Each dimension of the full-sized plane has been reduced 72 times for the model. Put another way, if 72 models of the aircraft were placed side by side, wingtip to wingtip, they would equal the wingspan of the original.

Scale can be expressed as a percentage where the description is easy to visualize – such as, "25 percent full size" when the model is reduced to a quarter of the full size. But the usual way of indicating scale is to show the exact proportion of the reduction: for example, 1:72 or 1/72 for the popular model aircraft scale.

While there are no hard-and-fast rules in modeling, modelers generally work in a constant scale when building up a collection. You might create a fleet of 1:72 scale aircraft because the charm and interest lies in comparing all of the different planes in your collection size for size, just as you would on a real airfield. Clearly if you make a diorama, everything on it must be to the constant scale for plausibility. A fighter pilot that stood taller than the aircraft would ruin the effect.

Selecting scale

In established modeling activities, such as model railroads, there are certain scales that have come to be

accepted over the years, and virtually everyone adheres to them. The scales span a wide range of sizes. For example, indoor railroads may go from 1:22.5 scale (or even larger) down to 1:220. In the larger scale, you would need both hands to lift a locomotive, and in the smaller, the locomotive would fit into a matchbox. Obviously you would choose the scale that suited your skill, space, time, and financial resources.

Though some model scales were scientifically calculated to give the best combination of size and detail accuracy, many of the long-established scales evolved in an arbitrary way. For example, the now universal 1:72 scale for model aircraft was arrived at in the 1930s by British modeler James Hay Stevens. He assumed that the lead soldiers he had bought were 1:36 scale (although they were actually 1:32 scale), and he halved that scale to make a more convenient size to fit a shelf – creating a scale of

1:72. He persuaded a company to construct wooden model aircraft kits to this size, and all other manufacturers that followed made their kits to the same scale.

The oldest model railroad scales came about in the same haphazard way. In the 1890s Märklin, who made the first tinplate train sets, scaled them to match the size of lead model soldiers and farm animals. This turned out to be 1:32 scale, and the gauge of the rails was 1¾in (45mm). It was called 1 gauge because it was the first to be formalized. Larger models became known as 2 gauge. When something smaller was required, a fairly arbitrary 1¼in (32mm) was chosen for the gauge which worked out at 1:43.5 scale, or ⁷⁄₁₆in (7mm) to 1ft (300mm). This was called 0 (zero) gauge. When demand developed for even smaller sets in the 1920s, the gauge was halved, the scale became ⅝in (16.5mm), ⁵⁄₁₆in (3.5mm) to 1ft

(300mm), and the result was termed "Half 0" – or HO.

Popular scales

There are a great many scales, and new scales are constantly being developed, often because a model manufacturer wants to create a new market. Here, we discuss the ones you are most likely to encounter and want to use.

Trains

Model railroads are produced to well-established scales, and the track gauges are usually linked with them. But gauges can vary, especially in the case of narrow-gauge models. To match actual cases, almost any plausible combination of scale and gauge is possible. Only the smaller scales and gauges suited for indoor use are covered here.

1:22.5 scale/G gauge The largest commercially produced size, depicting narrow-gauge trains on 1¾in (45mm) gauge track. Some scale variations are possible, depending upon the full-size gauge that 1¾in (45mm) is taken to depict.

1:32 scale/1 gauge Standard-gauge trains on 1¾in (45mm) gauge track. Sometimes 1:30 scale is used.

1:43.5 scale/0 gauge Standard-gauge trains on 1¼in (32mm) gauge track. In the United States, the scale used for this gauge is 1:48 (¼in (6mm) to 1ft), and in mainland Europe it is 1:45.

1:64 scale/S gauge Standard-gauge trains on ⅞in (22mm) gauge track. Popular in the United States.

1:76 scale/00 gauge This is a peculiar British variation on HO, where the body scale of the models is slightly enlarged but the models still run on ⅝in (16.5mm) gauge track, which is under-gauge for the scale. To correct this, some dedicated British

Above These three aircraft are the same type and size in real life but the size difference of the models is due to the different scales they are produced in. The largest scale used here is 1:32.

Above This bomber and fighter are both modeled in 1:72 scale. The difference in size is due to the fact that the real aircraft are equally different in size.

modelers alter the gauge to $^{23}/_{32}$in (18.2mm) (EM gauge) or $^{13}/_{16}$in (18.83mm) (P4/S4), which are accurate renditions of the gauge.

1:87 scale/HO gauge Standard-gauge trains on ⅝in (16.5mm) track. The most widely adopted scale in the world – about 80 percent of all railroad modelers use this gauge.

1:120 scale/TT gauge Standard-gauge trains on ½in (12mm) gauge track. There is a British variation of 1:103 scale running on ½in (12mm) gauge track, repeating the same scale/gauge error as noted with 00 gauge.

1:160 scale/N gauge Standard-gauge trains running on $^{11}/_{16}$in (9mm) gauge track (a scale of $^{1}/_{16}$in (1.9mm) to 1ft). After HO, this is the most popular scale. There is a British variation of 1:148 scale, and a Japanese variation of 1:150 scale on the same track gauge. Both of these give larger scale bodies on the same track gauge, and therefore offer a slightly inaccurate scale/gauge relationship.

1:220 scale/Z gauge Standard-gauge trains running on $^{9}/_{32}$in (6.5mm) gauge track – the smallest commercially supported model rail scale.

Narrow gauge There are many possible combinations. Typical is HOM, where models to 1:87 scale run on ½in (12mm) gauge track, depicting meter gauge. Similarly Nm uses 1:160 scale trains running on 6.5mm (Z) track depicting meter gauge trains. HOe has models to 1:87 scale running on 9mm (N) gauge track, depicting 750mm narrow gauge. There are numerous others, and in essence the scale is paired with the most appropriate gauge that is to be depicted.

In the United States the most common variations of narrow gauge, apart from G scale, are HOn2½ (using 9mm/N gauge track to depict 2ft 6in gauge), HOn3 (using 10.5mm – $^{13}/_{16}$in – gauge track to depict 3ft gauge), On2½ (using 16.5mm – ⅝in – HO track to depict 2ft 6in gauge), and On3 (using 19mm – ¾in – gauge track for 3ft gauge).

Aircraft

1:24 scale A limited number of giant "super kits" are made in this scale, covering the most famous fighting aircraft, such as the Spitfire, Stuka, and P–51 Mustang. Their size can make them vulnerable, but the completed models are most impressive.

1:32 scale Several manufacturers have plastic kits in this large scale, where every detail, inside and out, can be featured. As for the 1:24 scale, the finished models can pose a storage problem.

1:48 scale Sometimes known as "quarter scale": ¼in to 1ft (6mm to 300mm). This gives scope for fine detail on a larger model and is the next favorite scale after 1:72.

1:72 scale The most popular scale, with hundreds of plastic kits from many manufacturers. It is a convenient scale, working out at 6ft to 1 inch (180cm to 2.5cm).

1:144 scale Arrived at by halving 1:72 scale – therefore, 12ft to 1 inch (360cm to 2.5cm) – this gives very small models, which are easily stored and displayed.

1:200 scale The smallest scale, favored by collectors. Plastic kits and models of large airliners are often to this scale. Specialist suppliers make cast-metal aircraft (including fighters and bombers) at this scale, and these tiny models have exquisite charm.

Cars

1:18 scale Several super-detailed die-cast car ranges are made in this scale.

1:24 scale Some die-cast models and kits are available in this large scale.

1:32 scale Many plastic kits and some die-cast models are to this scale, which matches gauge 1 model trains.

1:43 scale The most popular size for die-cast automobiles, with many companies producing an ever-changing range of models at all prices. Some plastic and metal kits are also available. The scale matches European 0 gauge model trains.

1:87 scale Many American and European companies produce thousands of models in this scale, which matches HO trains. It has become a popular collecting scale in recent years, especially in continental Europe, even though the models were originally produced merely as rail accessories. There are numerous plastic kits and some metal ones. Heavy trucks and buses are popular in 1:87 scale. The models are well detailed but occupy minimal space.

Some 1:160 scale models are produced, in support of N gauge, and 1:120 road models are made for TT.

Military models

1:32 scale (also known as 54mm scale). This is the standard model soldier size, well supported, with ready-made, cast-metal, plastic, and kit models. AFVs are also modeled to this scale. Figures are 2⅛–2¼in high.

Model figures for collectors are also produced in 3¾in, 2¾in, 1½in, 1¼in, and 1in (90mm, 70mm, 40mm, 30mm, and 25mm) size, the smallest equating with HO and 00 gauge model railways. Many armored vehicle kits and models are available in 1:87 and 1:76 scale – the latter is favored by collectors of military vehicle models.

1:35 scale Though a slightly odd size, this is a well-established scale for large military vehicle models that originated in Japan. It is just below the 1:32/54mm scale that has been standard for model soldiers for over 100 years. Many plastic kits and accessories are available in this scale, and it is extremely popular for its bulk, fidelity, and high degree of detail.

Ships

Most ship models are made to fairly small scales. There is some variety among models made from plastic kits, because manufacturers tend to scale them to fit conveniently sized packages. However, the following are well established:

1:700 scale This scale was standardized by several Japanese kit-makers to produce a high-quality range of waterline warship models. There are numerous kits, and this is a good scale for the collector. A few models and kits are made to 1:720 scale, which is visually compatible in this small size.

1:600 scale This is a well-liked scale – 50ft to 1in (15m to 25mm) – with a fair range of plastic and wooden kits.

1:1200 scale This is a long-established "recognition" scale – 100ft to 1in (30m to 25mm) – favored by scratch-builders but also supported with some plastic kits.

There are also kits in 1:50, 1:150, 1:200, 1:300, 1:350, and 1:400 scale, among others.

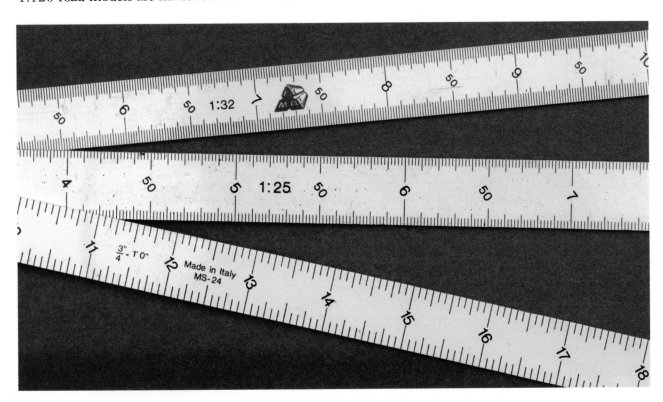

Left Scale rules can be bought so you can either measure the size from the model or convert the size dimension to the particular scale you require.

Structures

Styles of building are as varied as human culture, traditionally because of the suitability and performance of locally available materials. With improved communications and the development of trade, however, local materials became less significant for some types of structure. In certain cases this was a matter of prestige, while in others a readily transportable material came to be widely accepted: for a palace, Italian marble might be sent for, whereas more humble slate would be found roofing ordinary houses many miles from the quarries that supplied it. Wood is used throughout the world for doors, window frames, and floors. In certain areas and climates it is also used for the basic structure, although stone and brick are the norm in many regions of the world.

The performance of the materials used, especially their ability to withstand the elements, is a major factor in their selection. Another is the way in which their appearance changes over time; how a building weathers is an important part of its character, whether it is part of a townscape or an isolated farmstead.

The modelmaker who wants to achieve a realistic representation must choose materials that function effectively in structural terms, that can be easily and safely worked, give the desired appearance, and are readily and economically available. Nothing represents sawn, unpainted lumber better than wood itself. Brick and stone, on the other hand, are not usually suitable for the fabric of model buildings, mainly because of their weight and difficulty to model. To represent these materials, artifice is needed. This succeeds thanks to modern modeling clays and fillers, and the use of specialized painting methods.

Buildings
The house

This project demonstrates the building of a basic shell from foamboard. The same technique can be applied to more complex structures. Front and rear walls fit between two virtually identical gable end walls (one incorporating the side of a chimney). A single internal floor piece in the middle of the structure gives it strength and squareness, and allows the subsequent fitting of doors and windows.

Checklist

Materials

¼in (6mm) thick foamboard, Ruler, H or 2H pencil, Cutting mat, Try square, X-Acto handle and blades, Metal straight-edge, 1¼in (30mm) dressmaking pins, 1in (25mm) flat brush, ¼in (6mm) brush, White glue, Water, Screw-top jar, Damp cloth

Above The completed shell for a house. The finished shell has been painted before going on to model the roof and other details.

1 Make an accurate full-size drawing of the proposed house. This one was revised repeatedly until a satisfactory design was found. Indicate the position of the floor levels. Produce a second drawing by tracing over the first, showing the shapes and dimensions of the main parts. Allow for the thickness of the material used – in this case ¼in (6mm) thick foamboard.

2 Begin cutting out the main parts of the shell, using an X-Acto knife on a self-healing cutting mat. A blade with a ⅝in (16mm) straight cutting edge will slice cleanly through the foamboard. Pay great attention to getting all of the right-angled corners square and the sides straight with the aid of a metal ruler and a try square.

3 Draw lines on the inside of the wall pieces to show the floor levels. Insert the 1¼in (30mm) dressmaking pins in the areas that will form the top side of each butt joint. Push the points firmly into the foamboard but not completely through.

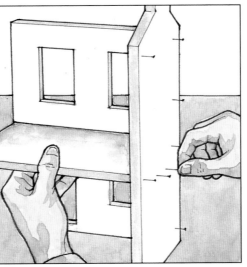

5 Glue the two edges of the center floor and fit it into position, using your penciled lines as a guide. Hold the floor in place with the pins.

7 Cut additional parts from foamboard to build up the thickness of the chimney, and provide a fitting ledge for the roof. This is necessary because the roof slope of this building is set inside the gable end walls. Glue and pin the chimney and roof supports into place.

4 Apply white glue to the face of one of the areas to be butt jointed. Stand the adjoining sides on a flat surface, and check that the corner is square. Push the appropriate pins in to hold the pieces while they adhere, but leave about ½–¾in (10–15mm) protruding. This allows them to be easily removed later. Use a thimble or bottle cork to push the pins without discomfort.

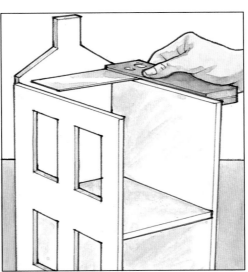

6 Glue and pin the back wall, once again checking the squareness of the structure, which should be done repeatedly as you progress. Attach the end wall in the same way to complete the assembly of the basic shell.

8 After about 10 minutes, remove the pins. Coat the entire structure with diluted white glue (about 75 percent glue to 25 percent water), applied with a 1in (25mm) flat brush. This seals the shell in preparation for the application of texture and detail, and prevents distortion. It is important to cover all surfaces, both interior and exterior.

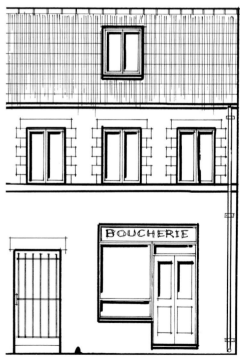

2 Pin and glue the main shell of the building. Cut the parts for the roof also in ¼in (6mm) foamboard and make a slot for the dormer window before fitting. The roof could be cut in one piece; two were used here to save wasting an offcut.

Above A basic foamboard building shell. At this stage no surface detail has been added.

The store

This model is in half relief – in other words, only the front is built. It is a three-story building, with a dormer window in the steeply pitched roof. On the first floor is a small store window, and to the side a gate gives access to a passage beneath the third floor. When the three floors are complete, a false back will be added to the structure.

Checklist

Materials

¼in (6mm) thick foamboard, Mat board, Ruler, H or 2H pencil, Cutting mat, Try square, X-Acto handle and blades, Craft knife, Metal straight-edge, 1¼in (30mm) dressmaking pins, 1in (25mm) flat brush, ¼in (6mm) brush, White glue, Water, Screw-top jar, Damp cloth

1 Make a full-size drawing and mark the parts on ¼in (6mm) foamboard. Cut the main shape, and the openings for doors and windows. Then cut the front wall, the two half-depth end walls, and three floor and ceiling pieces. The model will be in half relief at the back of a group of buildings, so it will only comprise the front half of the store and the forward slope of the roof.

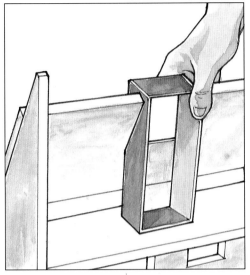

3 Build the dormer of mat board cut to fit the exact space, starting with one of the side pieces. Glue the dormer elements to each other and to the roof opening.

The brewery

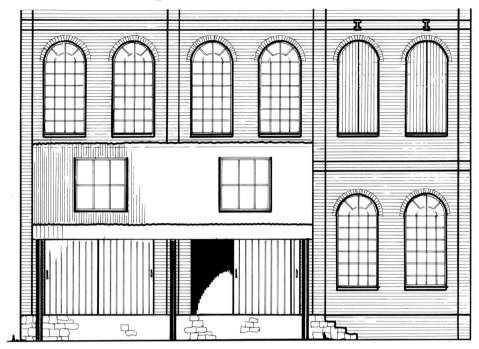

I Mark the parts on ¼in (6mm) foamboard according to a full-size drawing. Cut the principal shape, including doors and windows. The windows will come from a plastic kit, and their size must be carefully allowed for (including the thickness of the surface texture and detail to be applied later).

The impression of a large flat-roofed industrial building is achieved by selective compression. This is done by reducing the number of bays that would make up the façade, and by giving the illusion of a continuing series of identical openings. The resulting half-relief structure comprises two tall stories, and incorporates a loading dock, to be fitted with an awning, that protrudes from the front of the building.

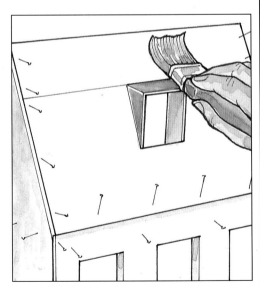

4 Add the rest of the roof, and coat the shell inside and out (including the mat board dormer) with a solution of 75 percent white glue and 25 percent water.

Checklist

Materials
¼in (6mm) thick foamboard, ⅛in (3mm) thick foamboard, Small length of "I" section polystyrene beam, Ruler, H or 2H pencil, Cutting mat, Try square, X-Acto handle and blades, Metal straight-edge, 1¼in (30mm) dressmaking pins, 1in (25mm) flat brush, ¼in (6mm) brush, White glue, Water, Damp cloth

2 Draw lines on the front of the shell to show where the brick piers will be. Their width was calculated to be an exact number of complete bricks. Assemble using the pinning and white glue method.

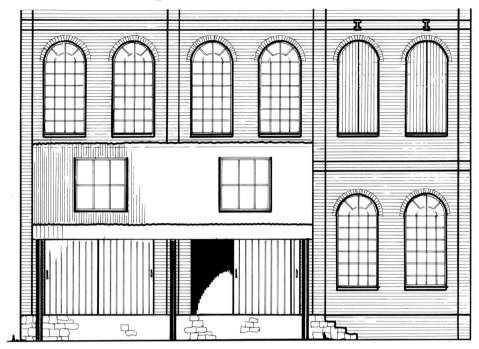

Above The completed shell of the brewery building.

3 The completed shell seen from the rear. This will be a flat-roofed half-relief model. A double thickness of foamboard is applied to the openings around the loading bay, and the loading platform floor is installed both in and outside the building.

4 Cut a section of plastic beam and make a hole for it at second floor level, where it will be needed for a loading pulley. Make sure that this is the correct size, then remove it and store it until later.

5 Add strips of ⅛in (3mm) foamboard as the basis of the brick piers in the front of the building. Coat the entire shell inside and out with a solution of 75 percent white glue/25 percent water, and pose it in its proposed site to check the overall proportions and visual balance.

Kit modification

Above The modified kit photographed from the rear. The walls have been thickened with foamboard, and a triangular false roof added.

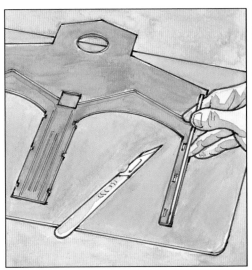

2 Using a craft knife, an X-Acto knife with a long, pointed blade, a metal ruler, and a self-healing cutting mat, begin reducing the height of the components. Strengthen the cut sections by gluing strips of styrene to the back. When a section of kit wall is trimmed to the correct size, cut an identical backing of ¼in (6mm) foamboard to give it realistic thickness.

It is not always necessary to make a shell from scratch. Here a plastic kit that included an attractive pair of arched openings is adapted to produce a single-story industrial building. The kit parts provide a ready-textured brick structure, but need to be reduced in height, and thickened around the openings. This is done with foamboard, which acts as a strengthening inner core. The building is planned to be served by a railroad track.

Checklist

Materials

¼in (6mm) thick foamboard, Selected parts of kit, Polystyrene solvent/glue, Cyanoacrylate glue, Ruler, H or 2H pencil, Cutting mat, Try square, X-Acto handle and blades, Craft knife, Metal straight-edge, 1¼in (30mm) dressmaking pins, 1in (25mm) flat brush, ¼in (6mm) brush, White glue, Water, Screw-top jar, Damp cloth

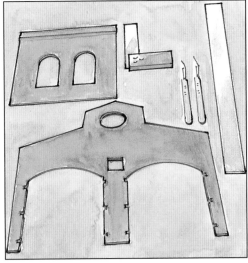

1 Plan a design using parts from a plastic kit, and pose them in their intended locations. Set out the components that need to be modified.

3 The two pieces of the kit, the foamboard wall section, and the necessary thickening around the doorways are added. The triangular piece of foamboard will be added at ceiling level to give strength. This will be a half-relief building on the diagonal.

Surface texture

Above Covering a building shell with modeling clay is a good way to create surface texture.

A simple, economical method of giving a building texture is to cover the shell with a layer of modeling clay. This can represent a rendered finish, or if suitably scribed, a brick- or stone-built wall. Rendering or brick in good condition will need a smoothed surface, but a stone wall can have a rougher texture. The modeling clay also conceals the joins in the foamboard shell.

Checklist

Materials
Modeling clay, Water. Fine sandpaper, Finishing paper

1 Pinch the modeling clay from the pack in small pieces. Here, white clay is used for a surface planned to be rendered and painted.

2 Press the pieces of clay into the surface of the building shell with your finger. Smooth the clay on with a circular motion, damping your finger with water as necessary. Make a layer about ⅟₁₆in (1mm) thick.

3 Cover all parts of the shell, including the chimney, with modeling clay.

4 The loading dock in front of this model was also coated in clay so that it can be scribed with stonework and paving. Terracotta-colored modeling clay was used on this building because it is to have a brickwork finish.

Surface detail

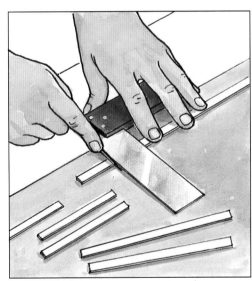

Above A completed shell, showing mounting board coated with modeling clay used to portray stone window and door sills.

5 A completed shell, entirely covered with modeling clay, is left to dry overnight. At this stage the surface is uneven: you can leave it like this to represent rougher stonework, or smooth it for brickwork, flat rendering, and dressed stone.

6 Smooth the dried modeling clay by rubbing down with fine sandpaper, followed by a finishing paper.

Create protruding parts of walls, moldings, windowsills, and steps by adding strips of mat board, which will later be covered in a layer of modeling clay. Carve or scribe brick- and stonework courses into the modeling clay on the main shell. Observe the details of different architectural styles, and pay careful attention to reproducing the correct sizes of bricks and stones, and to various types of bonding.

Checklist

Materials

Mat board, Modeling clay, Water, White glue, Ruler, H or 2H pencil, Cutting mat, Try square, X-Acto handle and blades, Metal straight-edge, ¼in (6mm) brush, Fine sandpaper, Flat needle file, Scriber, Damp cloth, Old toothbrush

I Cut strips of mounting board in suitable widths and lengths, using an X-Acto knife with a long pointed blade, a metal ruler, and a try square.

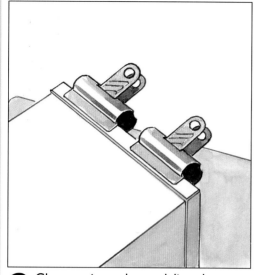

2 Glue a strip to the modeling clay surface of the shell with white glue. Clamp the joint with clothespins while it dries.

4 When you apply the first strip at a corner, cut it flush with one face. As you add strips, trim them carefully to fit at corners.

6 As the strips are added, and each face becomes less flat, the shell starts to look more interesting.

3 A strip that is trimmed to fit around a window or doorway must be fitted for size before gluing.

5 Diagonal trimming of the strips on the gable end will be done after the glue has dried.

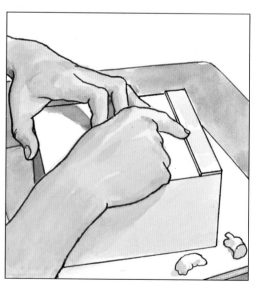

7 Cover the strips with a thin layer of modeling clay, and set aside to dry. Gently scrape away excess clay from areas that cannot be sanded, and remove it from corners with an X-Acto knife.

8 Use a flat needle file to restore the exact squareness of window and door openings distorted by the application of modeling clay.

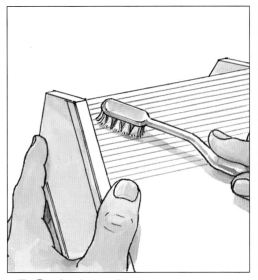

10 As the scribing progresses, remove the debris with a stiff brush. An old toothbrush is ideal for this.

9 To portray an area of exposed brickwork where the rendering has broken away, scribe horizontal courses into the dry clay, using a metal ruler and scriber. A scriber with a round handle is the easiest to maneuver.

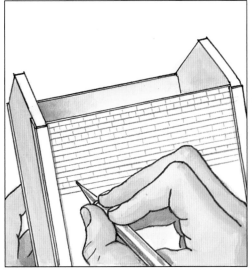

11 Add the vertical joints between bricks with the scriber. Here it is done freehand, but use a straight-edge if you prefer. Note that a particular type of brickwork bonding is reproduced in this example.

Above Carve or scribe brick- and stonework courses in the modeling clay. Pay careful attention to reproducing realistic sizes of bricks and stones.

Above Use strips of mat board to create protruding parts of walls, moldings, windowsills or steps. Then cover the mat board with modeling clay.

Windows and doors

Above The completed windows and doors play a major part in transforming the shell of a building into a realistic model.

Well-modeled doors and windows play a major part in transforming the shell of a building into a realistic model. They are often considered difficult to make because of the mistaken view that a frame must be modeled before the glass material is put in. Here we show a simple method of building up the frame on the plastic window material. It works equally well for windows and glass doors.

1 Cut a piece of clear styrene about ⅛in (3mm) larger all around than the doorway. Tape it temporarily in place on the inside of the building.

2 Glue a styrene strip of suitable square section (with the appropriate solvent) onto the front of the clear sheet, around the top and sides of the door opening. For a window, there would be a piece at the bottom also. Take care that the strips stick to the clear sheet and not to the shell.

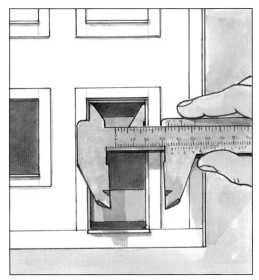

3 Check that the newly built door frame is square. Here, an inexpensive plastic caliper rule is used to ensure that the distance between the sides is constant top and bottom.

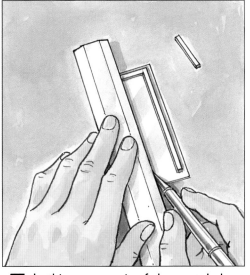

5 In this case, a pair of glass-paneled doors is being produced. Guidelines are lightly scored on the top face of the clear styrene, down the middle and across the bottom of the frame, to indicate where detail strips will be added.

7 Use different sizes of strip for the bars and other details. This door will have four clear panels at the top, with solid panels beneath – made by painting over the clear panels front and back. A solid door could be built up plank by plank on a thin sheet of regular styrene.

4 Untape the clear sheet with the frame stuck to it, so that you can do the rest of the work flat on the bench.

6 Working inside the frame, and on top of the clear sheet, use flat styrene strips to build up the door. Instal the verticals first, and fit the horizontals between them.

8 Build windows in the same way on clear styrene. These can include top lights. This technique is most useful for inward-opening windows. Mark the correct location of each completed door or window before setting it aside.

Outward-opening windows

Outward-opening windows cannot be modeled on a plastic window material base. Instead, the plastic is cut to the outer size of the opening part of the frame, and styrene strips are added behind it at the sides, top, and bottom to portray the frame. The strips form both the frame and the fixing area that attaches the window unit to the building shell.

Checklist

Materials

Clear styrene sheet, Styrene strip in various sizes, Styrene solvent, Cyanoacrylate glue, Masking tape, Plastic caliper rule, Ruler, H or 2H pencil, Cutting mat, Try square, X-Acto handle and blades, Metal straight-edge

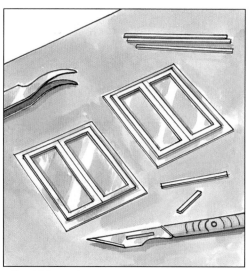

2 When the opening section is complete, apply wider strips of styrene to the back of the glazing to provide the frame and sufficient extra for fixing on the inside of the wall.

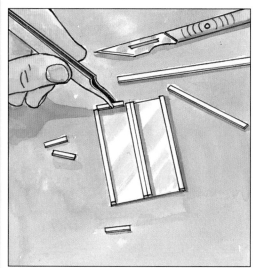

1 For an outward-opening window, build up the opening area on a piece of clear plastic of the exact size of the window. This is the size of the opening, less the width of the frame all around. For a pair of windows with a center opening, use a scribed line as a guide, and add vertical strips of styrene followed by horizontals.

3 Test tape the completed frames into place for a visual check, but remove for painting.

Other types of window

Large commercial windows can be built in the same way as domestic ones. The example shown here would in reality have comprised many small sheets of glass in separate frames. To model a modern style with expanses of uninterrupted glass, simply reduce the amount of framing. This project also illustrates the use of wooden frames, an alternative window style, and the construction of an old-fashioned name sign.

Checklist

Materials

Clear styrene sheet, Styrene strip in various sizes, Limewood strip, Styrene solvent, Cyanoacrylate glue, Masking tape, Gold enamel paint, Black cardboard, Wood stain, Light box, Ruler, H or 2H pencil, Cutting mat, Try square, X-Acto handle and blades, Metal straight-edge, Stencil or computer, Small good-quality brush

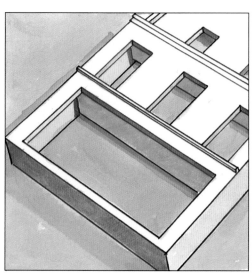

1 Make a large opening in the shell to accommodate the café front. It occupies almost all of the front of the building at ground level. This is a shallow, half- or low-relief model, so the shell is open at the rear. The lack of depth will be disguised by painting.

Above The finished café window with the sign above.

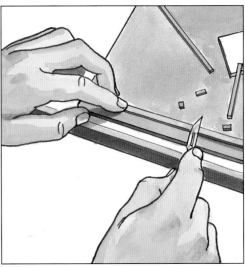

4 Test the unit in the opening. Fix any problems of fit around the edges by sanding or scraping back the outer frame.

2 Tape a piece of clear plastic over the window area on your full-size drawing of the model. The plastic needs to be about ⅛in (3mm) larger all around than the opening. Build the framing onto the plastic in the same way as for house doors and windows. In this case the frame will have a stained finish, so a suitable stripwood (lime, not balsa) is used. Scrape and sand the stripwood to size if necessary.

3 Add the paneling under the windows and in the lower door panels, and when the café front is complete, untape it from the drawing.

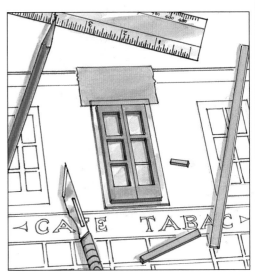

5 Build the inward-opening second-floor windows in a similar way on the drawing. Glue the windows into position and stain with a fine brush.

6 Produce the lettering for the café sign in a suitable size on a home computer and print it. Alternatively, you could use a stencil. Place it face down on a light box so that you can clearly see it in reverse. Tape a strip of clear plastic of the exact size on top.

Above For true authenticity, this barn door has been modeled with weathered and battered wood.

7 Trace the lettering (in reverse) in gold enamel paint. Obviously, this requires a steady hand. When the paint is dry, place a strip of thin black cardboard behind the lettering, and build a stained stripwood frame around the unit.

Above The windows have been fixed into the building on the inside and then a thin inner wall added to prevent them falling out. This inner wall is then locked in place by adding a cross wall. These are made from mat board and painted.

House roofs

Above The house and roof in its final form.

2 This roof fits inside the gable ends of the building. Check the strips already fitted inside the building to support the roof, and add padding pieces if necessary.

In this section the roof is added to the house shell, along with gutters, downspouts, and chimney details. The materials are styrene and mat board, with the addition of readily obtainable scrap metal and two-part epoxy putty. In this case, a tiled roof is portrayed, but the same procedure can be used for other overlapping materials.

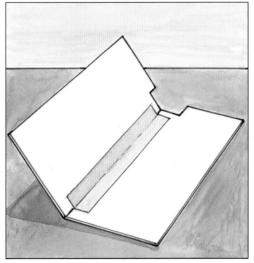

1 Cut two pieces of mat board to form the slopes of the roof, and attach them with a strip of masking tape on the underside. Make a cut out at one end to accommodate the chimney.

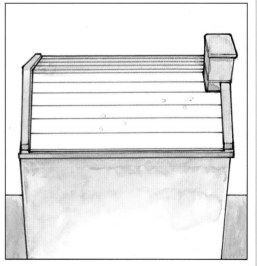

3 Rule lines across the roof section to guide the positioning of the roofing material. Space the lines carefully to allow for the overlap of the model slates, tiles, or shingles to be applied. Attach the roof section with white glue.

4 Ridged styrene sheet is used to represent the roof tiles. Cut it into horizontal strips, allowing sufficient depth for the exposed tile plus the portion overlapped by the row above. Starting at the bottom, glue the first strip to the roof, with a spacing strip underneath, using styrene solvent. Allow for an overhang at the base of the roof, so that the bottom edge of the tiles will cover the line where the guttering will be fixed.

6 Glue styrene strip over the ends of the umbrella rib with cyanoacrylate glue. When these are dry, trim them to the shape of the "U" section, and fix the lengths of gutter to the building along the roof edge. This structure has a corbeled section rendered like the rest of the building.

8 Attach small pieces of styrene strip to the wall with cyanoacrylate glue to form the fixing brackets for the downspout, which is then glued into place. Use cyanoacrylate at the top of the umbrella rib and fix the rest with styrene solvent.

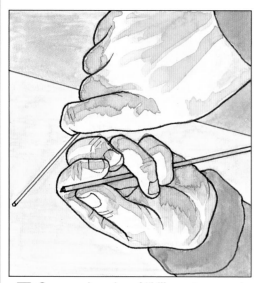

5 Cut two lengths of "U" section metal to the length of the building – ours were salvaged from the ribs of an old umbrella. File the ends square with a needle file.

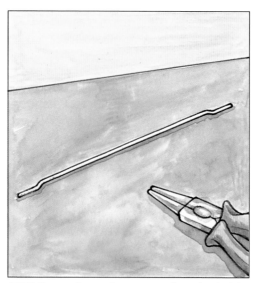

7 Cut a piece of styrene tube of suitable diameter to form the downspout: the length is the height of the gutter from the base of the building. Bends are needed at each end, to clear the protruding section at the bottom, and to allow for the overhang of the gutter at the top. Form the bends with round-nosed pliers to avoid damaging the styrene tube.

9 Bind small lengths of electrical insulation tape around the pipe at each bracket. Add the door handle – in this case a round one formed from a pin with a spherical head. Cut off most of the shank with side cutters, and fix the remaining length with cyanoacrylate into a small hole drilled in the door.

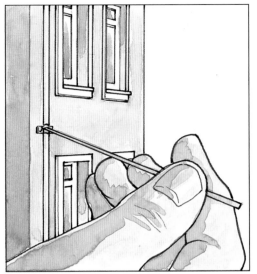

10 Simulate the heads of the bolts holding the brackets to the wall by carefully applying blobs of white glue. If these do not seem large enough at first, allow them to dry, and make a second application.

12 Glue the sections of ridge tiles along the top of the roof with styrene solvent, leaving a slight gap between each one.

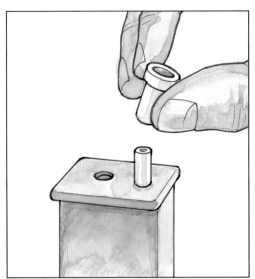

14 Cut two smaller pieces of styrene tube of a diameter that will fit tightly inside the pipes at the top of the chimney and act as fixing pegs. Make holes to suit these in the top of the chimney. Fix the pegs into place with cyanoacrylate glue, and attach the chimney pipes to them with styrene solvent.

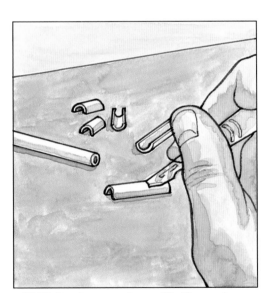

11 Produce sections of half-round ridge tile from styrene tube of suitable section. Slice a piece down the middle and cut lengths off. Half-round styrene section can be used to make the task easier.

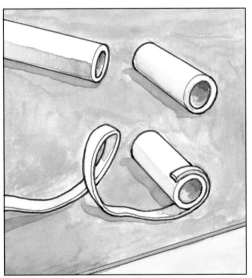

13 Cut more styrene tube for the pipes that fit on top of the chimney. In this case there are two of exactly the same length. Form the beading around the top with a circle of very fine styrene strip. Pre-curve it by drawing it sharply between your thumbnail and forefinger.

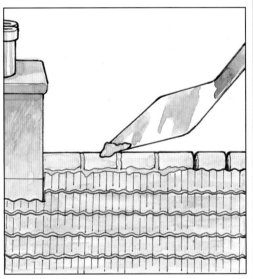

15 Mix some two-part epoxy putty and apply it with a palette knife to the joints between the sections of ridge tile, and to their lower edges. Wet the palette knife blade if necessary to improve the spreadability of the putty. Some of the surplus can be removed immediately with a damp cloth, and the rest carved off when dry with a fine craft knife blade or a dental probe. Allow 24 hours for drying.

16 Apply epoxy putty in a similar way to the top of the chimney to provide the haunching in which the chimney pipes are bedded.

18 Cut strips of lead foil to form the roof flashing. This is the foil found around the tops of some wine bottles, not the thinner foil used for cooking or for candy wrappers.

17 Give the roof an undercoat of red/brown paint. Add enough talcum powder to some modeling enamel to create a thin, matte, textured slurry. When dry, this perfectly reproduces the appearance of non-glazed tiles.

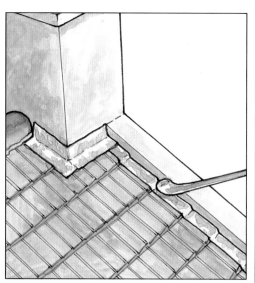

19 Apply the final paint finish to the roof using dry brush technique. Attach the flashing around the edge of the chimney end where the tiles meet the gable end walls.

Diagonal roof slates

Roof materials and styles vary considerably. These slates applied in a diagonal pattern are typical of parts of Europe, and would therefore be suitable for some World War II dioramas. The slates can be represented by heavy colored paper or thin cardboard. Success largely depends on the accurate drawing of the diagonal grid on the roof.

Checklist

Materials
Colored heavy art paper, White glue, ¼in (6mm) glue brush, H or 2H pencil, Cutting mat, Craft knife, Metal straight-edge, Damp cloth

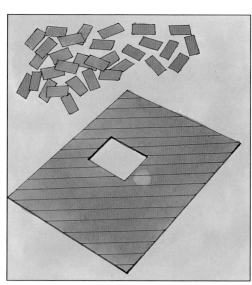

1 Cut a piece of dark gray or black heavy art paper to fit the area you are slating. This building is in half relief so only one roof slope is needed. Draw 45° diagonal guidelines in pencil on the paper, spacing them by the width of the slates. Cut the slates from the same material in rectangles twice as long as wide. Although you can calculate how many you will need, it is more convenient in practice to prepare them in batches as you go along.

Above The dormer window in the roof of the store building.

4 Create the third row of slates in the same way, reverting to the direction of the first diagonal. Continue the procedure until you have covered the entire roof.

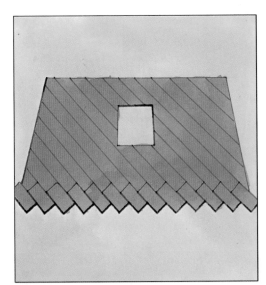

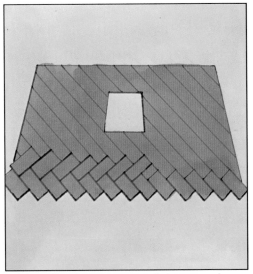

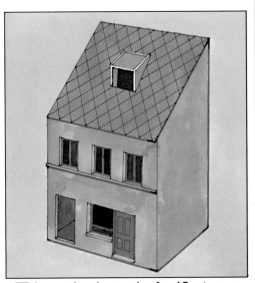

2 Starting at the bottom, fix the first row of slates into place with white glue. Each slate must be set diagonally (in this case, sloping top left to bottom right), with the center point of the bottom long edge forming the overlap point at the edge of the roof.

3 Apply the next row of slates on the opposite diagonal (top right to bottom left), overlapping the first row by half a unit, so that the lower slate forms a square.

5 Leave the glue to dry for 15 minutes. Then turn the piece over and trim off the surplus around the edges of the roof and the dormer window with a knife. To complete it, the roof will need gutters, ridge detail around the dormer, and a painted finish.

Wooden structures

When modeling structures built of unpainted wood, nothing is more effective than wood itself. This project constructs the frame for an awning over a freight bay on a brewery building. It is made from stripwood of the type and size readily available from many hobby stores.

Checklist

Materials
Various sizes of stripwood, A cork tile, Cyanoacrylate glue, Pins or brads, H or 2H pencil, Try square, Ruler, Dressmaking pins, Narrow plastic tube, Razor saw, Side cutters, Fine drill bit, Pin chuck

Above The completed wooden structure provides a good support for roofing.

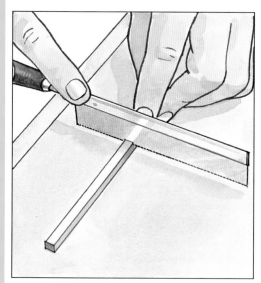

1 Begin with one of the triangular sections of vertical framing at one end of the structure. Cut a piece of stripwood to length, using a razor saw whose small teeth carve an end that looks in scale.

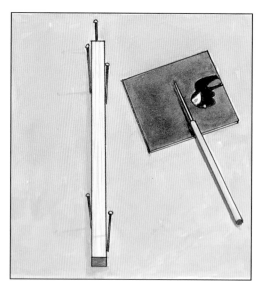

2 Place the piece on a cork tile, and hold it in position by means of a row of pins down either side of it. Cut a thicker piece of stripwood to form an upright. Put a small amount of cyanoacrylate glue on a scrap of cardboard, and make an application tool from a pin fixed into the end of a length of narrow plastic tube.

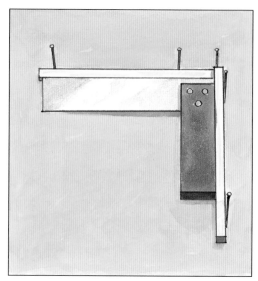

3 Set the second strip of wood on the cork at right angles to the first, using a try square to ensure accuracy. Stick pins along the outside of the upright piece.

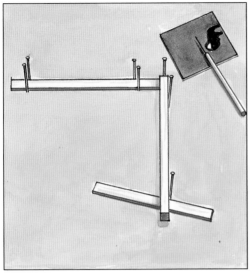

4 Slide a spare length of stripwood under the free end of the upright piece, and attach the two parts of the frame with a small amount of cyanoacrylate glue. The row of pins ensures that the joint is a right angle.

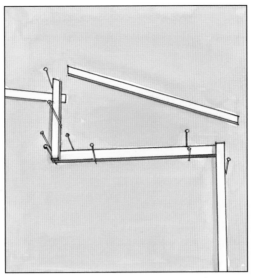

6 A diagonal piece is now to be added. Cut it to length, making an angle at each end. Mark a line in the top of the upright to indicate where it will be notched.

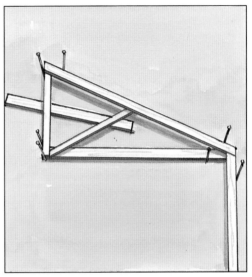

8 Notch one end of the diagonal into the thicker upright, and the other on top of the relevant piece, and adhere with cyanoacrylate glue. Cut a sub-diagonal and glue it in place. Again, use a spare scrap of wood to act as a spacer underneath.

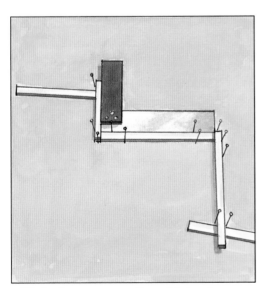

5 In the same way, fix a third strip at a right angle to the free end of the first piece.

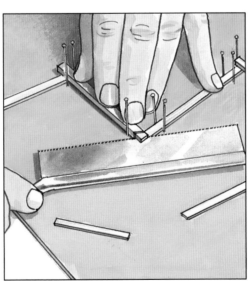

7 Cut the line of the notch to a suitable depth in one plane, using the razor saw. Cut the notch in the other plane to remove a tiny chip of wood that can be discarded.

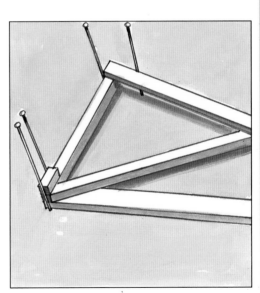

9 Note the addition of a small block, which will aid the fixing of the frame squarely to the building.

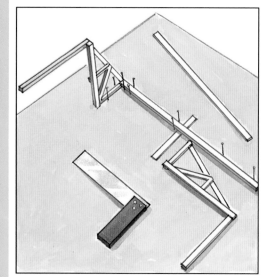

10 Build an identically sized frame in mirror image to the first. This will form the opposite end of the structure. Cut three strips of wood the length of the roof to represent horizontal beams. Pin the first frame to the cork sheet, and fix the first horizontal beam to it, as shown. Again, the pins and the try square ensure a right angle joint.

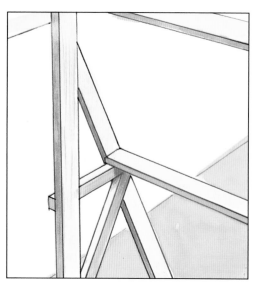

12 The joint for the second beam looks like this.

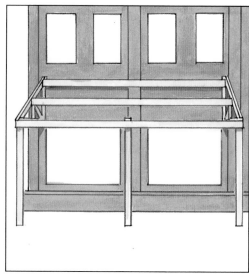

14 When all the pieces are in place, position the structure in front of the building to which it will be fixed.

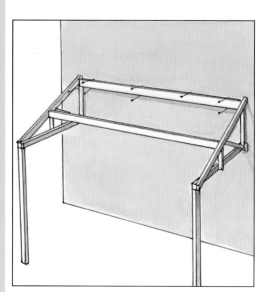

11 Attach the other end of the structure with glue, and add the second beam.

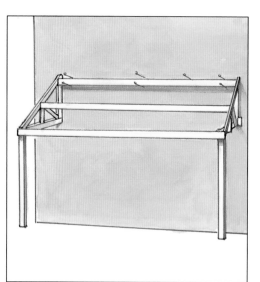

13 Attach the third beam and cut a third upright to fit in the center front.

15 As the freight bay is to be served by a railroad spur, and there are other tracks in a crowded area, it is important to check that there is sufficient clearance all around.

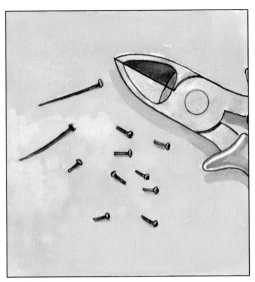

16 Use side cutters to remove the point and most of the shank from some small brads or pins – ours are the type sold for fixing down railroad tracks.

Above This warehouse has been detailed using pieces of stripwood. Note the finishing details such as the cross-bracing effect on the inside of the warehouse doors.

17 With a fine bit and pin chuck, drill holes where bolts would be inserted to hold a real structure together. Glue the pinheads into the holes with cyanoacrylate.

Left The pulley used to detail this warehouse building was a commercial item, supplied by a model boat store. Simple wooden brackets have been made to attach the pulley to the building.

Corrugated iron roof

Above The completed corrugated iron awning on the wooden frame. Notice the painting to indicate the effects of weathering and rust.

This simulation of a corrugated iron roof is designed to be built onto a wooden frame. When complete, the entire structure fits onto the front of the brewery building modeled earlier. The roof consists of overlapped sheets of thin styrene sold for this purpose, and is very convincing in conjunction with the wooden construction that supports it.

Checklist

Materials

Corrugated styrene sheet, Styrene solvent, Cyanoacrylate glue, Pins or brads, H or 2H pencil, Try square, Ruler, X-Acto handle and blade, Fine bradawl, Pin to apply glue, Side cutters

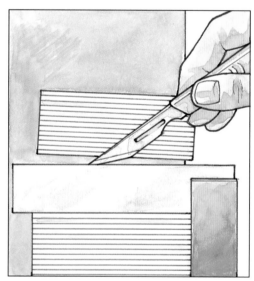

1 Cut a sheet of the thin styrene that represents corrugated iron into strips suitable to a scale of around 6–8ft (2–2.5m) in length. Then cut the strips the other way to simulate sheets about 3ft (1m) wide. Use a try square to make sure that the sheets are rectangular.

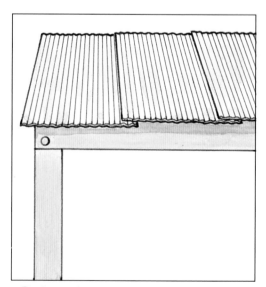

2 Begin at a bottom corner of the roof. Fix the first sheet of styrene to the wooden frame with cyanoacrylate glue, allowing a suitable overhang at the side and the front. Apply the second sheet alongside it, overlapping by two corrugations. Adhere it to the wood with cyanoacrylate, and to the styrene with styrene solvent. Continue the process along the lower part of the roof, until you reach the end. Cut the last sheet if necessary to provide a symmetrical overhang.

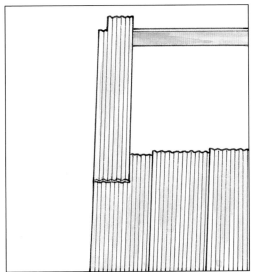

3 Begin the upper layer. Cut the first sheet down the middle, so that the vertical lines of joints do not coincide. In this case, a corner was also removed to clear part of the brickwork of the building. Position the sheet so that the bottom overlaps the top of the lower row.

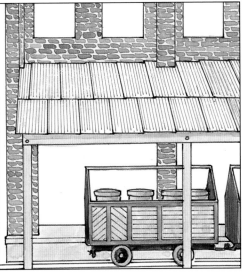

5 Check the structure is in position against the building to ensure that it fits correctly and that there is adequate clearance for the railroad cars.

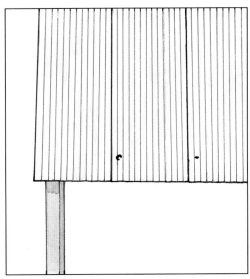

7 Remove the points and most of the shank from some small brads or pins, using side cutters. Fix the resulting bolt heads into the roof holes with cyanoacrylate glue.

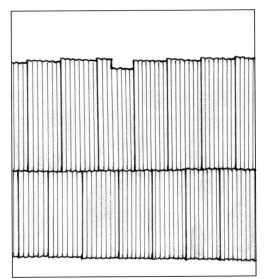

4 Complete the upper layer in the same way as the lower, until the roof looks like this. The cutout in the center is again to clear part of the building.

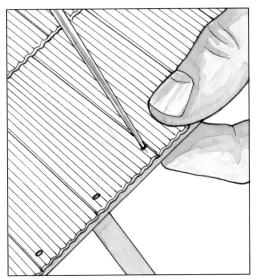

6 Following the line of the wooden frame beneath, and where two sheets overlap, pierce a series of small holes with a bradawl.

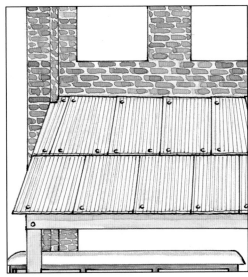

8 Repeat the application of the bolt heads along all the joint lines of the roof.

Detailing a building

Above The completed building showing detailing and the varied effect of hand-scribed brickwork.

Every building needs detailing in order to make a realistic model. You can improvise with the materials that you use. Here we have used parts from a kit, sheet styrene, stripwood, and some small components originally intended for a ship.

1 Plastic arched windows from a kit are suitable for adding detail to the brewery building modeled earlier. Carefully brush the front of each window with an appropriate model paint. Treat the visible parts of the molding only – not the back.

2 Prepare all of the windows in the same way, and set them aside to dry.

3 Cut some clear plastic sheet to the shape of the windows.

5 The large sliding doors to the freight bay are produced from a piece of sheet styrene cut to the relevant size. Cut pieces of stripwood to the same length, and adhere them to the styrene with cyanoacrylate glue.

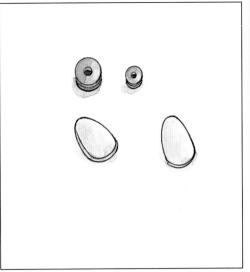

7 You could use a commercial pulley block, but this one was improvised. A collection of small ship parts provided two small wooden pulleys, and some pieces of sheet styrene, cut to shape, were added.

4 Use styrene solvent to glue the clear plastic sheet to the back of the window frame moldings.

6 On the upper floor there is a doorway for taking in sacks via a pulley block on a bracket. Make the door frame by cutting away the inner web from one of the window frame moldings. Form a pair of round-topped doors from stripwood on a styrene base as in Step 5.

8 These items were fixed together with a shaft and mounting link of 30 thou brass wire, using cyanoacrylate glue.

Harbors

A harbor can be a diorama in its own right as a way of displaying several different models together: buildings, ships, road, or rail vehicles, and quayside artifacts. But it is also popular on model railroad layouts, where a harbor focuses on a form of traffic interchange – sea to rail. Though you could not model a huge modern ocean terminal (except, perhaps, in tiny scale), harbors come in many sizes, and because they vary so much you can make a model to fit whatever space you have available.

Harbors make attractive scenic models and are especially suitable for railroad layouts. This German harbor serves both fishing and general commerce.

Checklist

Materials

Modeling knife, Small saw, Glues, Other conventional tools and materials, including sheets of embossed plastic or cardboard, Stone, Brick, or Wood facings, Balsa wood and/or Stripwood, Hardboard or plastic sheet

1 The easiest way to make a harbor outline – whether in a model railroad baseboard or a board for a diorama – is simply to saw out the desired shape in the board. Glue or pin a sheet of smooth plastic or hardboard underneath the resulting aperture to represent the water surface.

2 Paint and varnish the surface to depict water. Cut the harbor or jetty wall facings from strips of stone/brick/wood sheet of suitable depth, and glue them all around the cut out edges of the board. Stripwood uprights to portray rubbing strakes are optional. In small scales, matchsticks can be used for uprights.

3 Materials used for harbor or jetty wall facings vary considerably. Apart from stone, stone blocks, or brick, you might find wood facing in older or smaller harbors, or steel piling in modern or modernized harbors.

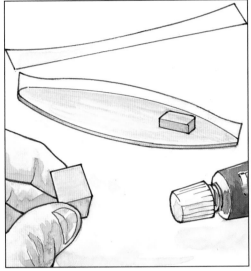

4 There are numerous wood or plastic kits of boats which can be used on harbor layouts, though in some cases, they may need to be cut down to waterline depth. Fishing boats or simple scows can easily be made from balsa wood and paper.

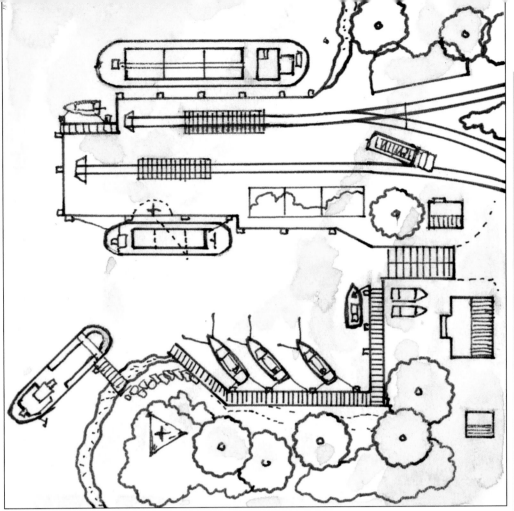

5 A suggested scheme for a harbor layout. The model includes scows and a yacht marina, along with buildings, giving big scope for modeling.

6 Here is an ambitious harbor scheme, with a kit-built wood coaster, a neatly paved jetty, steel-pile facing, and a narrow-gauge railroad.

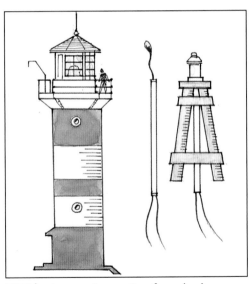

7 An interesting option for a harbor on the coast is the addition of a small lighthouse or a beacon on one corner of the sea wall. Here are two typical examples, both available in kit form but easy to build from scrap wood or cardboard. A real miniature light bulb can be wired in to provide a flashing light.

Modeling an airbase

Above A F–4E Phantom undergoing maintenance inside a hangar.

I Workbenches abound in hangars. Large ones will be against the walls, but some small ones can be moved closer to the aircraft. These are fairly simple items with legs braced with bars to keep them firm and sturdy enough to support large pieces of machinery. Note the lip around the edges to stop bits rolling off.

In real life an aircraft is seldom left unattended, so some modelers prefer to put their airplane on a base and surround it with activity. All sorts of ground equipment can be found on an airbase – starter vehicles, a loader for bombs and missiles, and ground crew operating these. Quite a lot of machinery is available in model form, but there is plenty that you can make yourself. The example here is an F–4E Phantom undergoing maintenance, and because so much of the aircraft is uncovered, the scene is set inside a hangar. The two walls representing a corner of the maintenance bay are constructed from ribbed plastic sheeting, with pillars from square tubing, and the scene is mounted on a piece of chipboard big enough to take the aircraft. The materials can be purchased from most good hobby stores, and photographs from aircraft books will be useful for reference. The measurements are for 1:48 scale.

Checklist

Materials

30 thou (0.75mm) plasticard, Various sizes of plastic strip and rod, Ribbed plastic sheeting, Plastruct fineline perforated shapes, Sharp knife, Razor saw, Sanding block, Metal ruler, Scriber

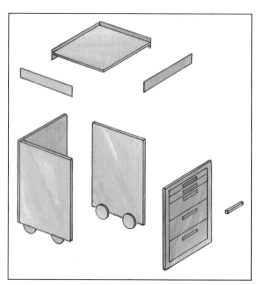

2 Aircraft are maintained with tools designed for each type, which are normally kept in specific tool chests with many drawers and on wheels. Cut the sides of the chest from plasticard, and scribe the front panel to represent the drawers. Remember to cut the top to the correct size, and make the lip with strip, as before. Attach small disks of 1/8in (3mm) plastic rod to represent wheels.

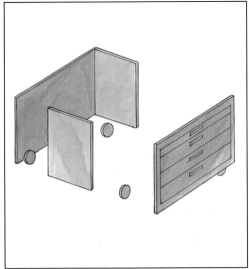

3 A longer chest holds tools for bigger jobs. Again cut four sides to size, and scribe the drawers on the front. Add handles to both chests, made from 1/64in (0.5mm) strip. Butt joint all of the sides, and rub them down with fine sandpaper when hard. Cut the top out, and add a lip cut from strip.

5 Casters are also needed on the small wheeled cart. This is used to transport parts from the plane to the main workbench or for any similar purpose. Its handrails can be made from flower arranging wire.

7 The steps are constructed from Plastruct A2 angle and tread plate molded plasticard, cut to the sizes shown. The handrail consists of 60 thou (1.5mm) rod, cold bent to shape. Do not forget the wheels on the rear, which are situated so that when the steps tilt backward they come into contact with the ground for ease of movement.

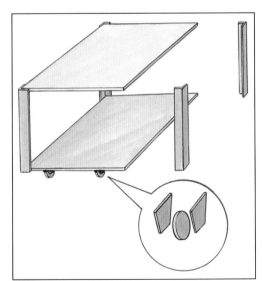

4 The two-tier stand is basically a mobile bench, and can be used anywhere. It would carry tools and machinery, so find some small unused kit parts to place on it. Cut the shelves to the size you want, and add caster wheels to the base, as shown in the diagram.

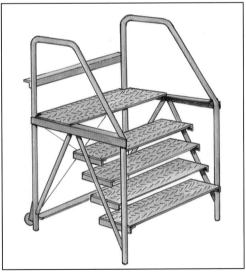

6 The ladder gives access to panels on the aircraft, which can be fairly high. It consists of steps leading to a wide platform to enable the ground crew to work safely. The handrails extend above the platform to provide a guardrail for the technician.

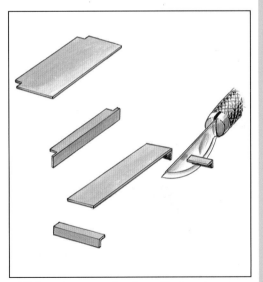

8 Let the steps harden off, then bend both handrails to match. Attach the steps to one side only, making sure that they are equidistant and at 90°. When they are nearly hard, add the other side and cement each step with care. Stand the piece on a flat surface and check that everything is square and level.

Airfields

Above The scope for airfield modeling is enormous. A very large model such as this 1:24 scale Junkers 57 "Stuka," can be displayed as if in the corner of a hangar, with every conceivable detail of overhaul incorporated.

2 An interesting airfield variation is a diorama featuring a forward combat area with the aircraft under camouflage cover, figures in combat clothing, and possibly even troops and a patrol car guarding the landing zone.

The options when modeling airfields are considerable. An airfield, or part of an airfield, can make an interesting addition to a large model railroad layout. But even more importantly, an airfield diorama or background is the perfect way of displaying model aircraft in realistic surroundings. An airfield model also makes an ideal background for model aircraft photography. Since even the smallest real airfield is a large place, you can normally only model part of it, or some specialized aspect, such as the area around a hangar. But any approach you choose should seek to create the atmosphere of the real environment.

I The most usual and straightforward way of building a model airfield base is to use thick plywood or chipboard of the size that fits your space, but at least 15in x 22in (38cm x 55cm). A model railroad backscene, showing distant countryside, can be glued to the backboard, which is best made from a strip of plywood or hardboard at least 6in (150mm) deep.

Checklist

Materials

Grass mat or grass scenic flock powder, Model trees and bushes, Plywood or chipwood, Scenic backgrounds, Buildings to choice or cardboard or wood for making them, Modeling tools, Model paints, Cardboard or printed paper road surface for runways, ramps, etc.

4 A more ornate development is to model sufficient depth of hangar for the aircraft to be placed partly inside. On this attractive Junkers 52 diorama, the hangar is made from cardboard and wood, the base from chipboard, and runway beacons from beads. Passengers and crew add to the interest.

3 Mark out a cardboard sheet to represent the tarmac (in this case for a heliport). Use grass mat, or grass flock powder sprinkled over glue, for the grass areas.

5 Another interesting variation is to model part of an aircraft carrier flight deck to display a selection of naval airplanes. You can depict the catapult, exhaust deflectors, deck crew, and an aircraft ready to launch, with others in line.

Stockade scene

Above The finished stockade scene. The representation of the light snow covering on the ground is particularly effective.

This project portrays the entrance to a typical 19th-century North American stockade. The scene is designed to be viewed from the front (outer side), so only the area of the gateway is modeled. The season chosen is winter, so we show a technique for representing snow. The scale is 1:32.

Checklist

Materials

Dried straight twigs about ¼in (6mm) diameter, ½in (12mm) thick chipboard, Expanded polystyrene tiles, Small-section stripwood, Modeling clay, Styrene strip and tube, Brass rod, White glue, Cyanoacrylate glue, Two-part epoxy glue, Brown (household) latex paint, White acrylic paint, Sawdust, Spackle compound, Foil from top of a wine bottle, Small brads, H or 2H pencil, Fine-grade sandpaper, Hot glue gun, Cutting mat, Craft knife, Metal straight-edge, Small hammer, 1in (25mm) brush for white glue, Palette knife, Damp cloth

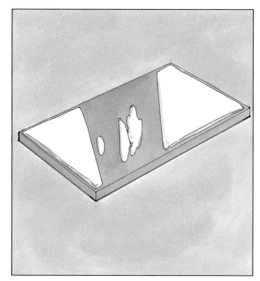

1 Cut a chipboard base measuring 12 × 6in (300 × 150mm) and sand the edges smooth. Mark the area of the dirt road, and fix pieces of expanded polystyrene tile on either side of it with a hot glue gun. Stick smaller pieces on the track itself to give slight surface undulation.

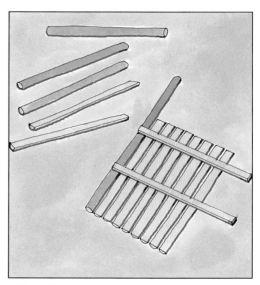

2 Select and prepare some dried straight twigs to model the rough-cut lumber (split logs) of the stockade's outer wall. Choose pieces about ¼in (6mm) in diameter, cut them along their length, and assemble as shown. Glue the twigs together with cyanoacrylate glue. Repeat this process for the other side of the gateway.

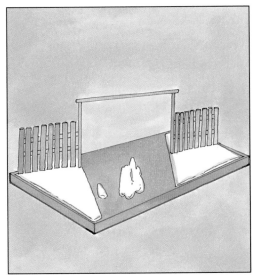

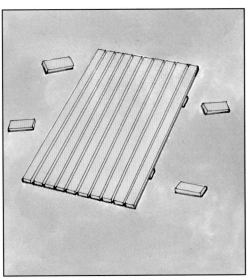

3 Fix the wall sections to the base with two-part epoxy glue, and add the bar over the gateway. To look realistic, the height of the gateway was calculated to allow the passage of mounted figures and horse-drawn wagons.

5 Make the gates for the stockade in the same way as the walls, but entirely in small-section stripwood. Cut the two main horizontal pieces of each gate longer than needed and tape them to the work surface. The vertical planks are about ¼in (6mm) wide. Cut them slightly shorter than the wall pieces, and glue them in place with cyanoacrylate glue.

7 Trim the horizontal pieces to the width of the gate. Repeat the procedure for the second gate.

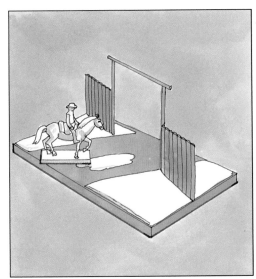

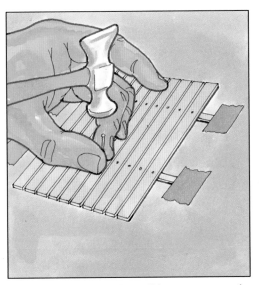

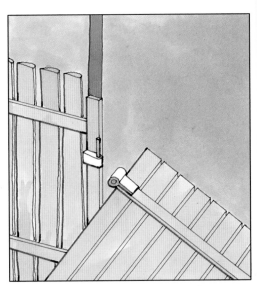

4 Position the mounted figure temporarily on the base to check the overall balance and composition of the scene. This was considered satisfactory.

6 Use a brad and small hammer to make indentations in the planks along the lines of the horizontals to represent nails.

8 There are two hinges on each gate. Each hinge has two halves consisting of a section of styrene strip with a piece of styrene tube fixed to the end. Attach the upper half of each hinge to the edge of the gate horizontals, and the lower halves at a suitable height to stripwood posts added to the ends of the walls. For maximum strength, make all these joints with cyanoacrylate glue rather than styrene solvent.

9 Glue short lengths of brass rod into the tubes on the lower parts of the hinges to form the pins. Mount the gates temporarily to check the fastening.

11 Build up the level of the ground in the gap between the expanded polystyrene and the base of the wall, using modeling clay.

13 Set the model aside for 24 hours to allow it to dry.

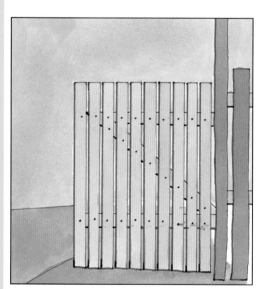

10 Add diagonal supports of stripwood to the rear of each gate, and simulate nail fixings as in Step 7. Check the appearance of the gates in position.

12 Make an earth mix of brown latex paint, spackling compound, white glue, and sawdust, and spread it over the base and the newly modeled ground levels with a palette knife. Be careful to ensure a rough finish. Before the mixture starts to set, plant blades of grass in it along the edge of the wall.

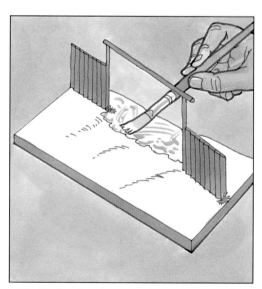

14 Apply white acrylic paint over the earth mix in the area to be covered by snow. When it is dry, brush white glue over it.

15 Load some commercial snow powder onto a palette knife and sprinkle it onto the glue by gently tapping the knife.

17 Glue the strips with cyanoacrylate over the top of the gateposts to form straps. Fix a suitably sized pin or small brad into a hole in each strap with cyanoacrylate .

16 Cut two strips from the heavy foil top of a wine bottle.

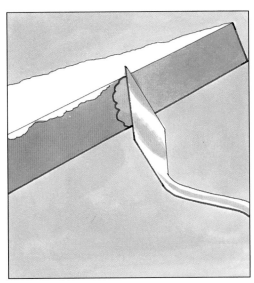

18 Fill the edge of the chipboard with spackle. When it is dry, sand the edge to present a neat finish.

Above Here a piece of model terrain is being coated with a thin coat of white glue.

Above Commercial snow powder, or alternatively baking powder, is applied onto white glue. A good way of applying the powder is to use a pipette.

Trench scene

Unlike many military installations that sit on the landscape, this scene is by its very nature cut into the ground. It takes the form of a shallow vertical section through the earth, showing the trench and a dugout. Simple materials are used for the basic structure and for posts, fencing, corrugated iron, and sandbags. Duckboards, barbed wire, and the figures are additional details.

Checklist

Materials

¼in (6mm) thick plywood, ½in (12mm) thick chipboard, ¼in (6mm) thick foamboard, Power jig saw or coping saw, Fine sawdust, Small-section stripwood, Corrugated styrene sheet, Expanded polystyrene, Crystals to simulate water (e.g. E-2 water), Household filler powder, Styrene solvent, White glue, Glue sticks, H or 2H pencil, Cutting mat, X-Acto handle and blades, Metal straight-edge, Dressmaking pins, Plastic container for earth mixture, Container for heating crystals (e.g. food can), Palette knife, ¼in (6mm) brush

Above The finished trench scene. At this stage, there is still work to be done on improving presentation.

1 Build the infrastructure for the scene from shaped pieces of ¼ in (6 mm) thick plywood attached around a base of ½in (12mm) thick chipboard with white glue and nails. Cut the pieces with a power jig saw, or by hand with a coping saw. The scale is 1:32.

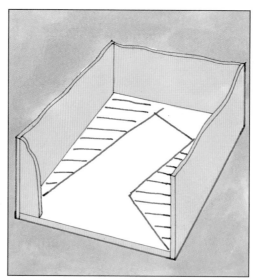

2 Draw the outline of the trench on the base board, indicating the area to be occupied by the dugout.

3 Use an X-Acto knife with a fine pointed blade to cut the ¼in (6mm) thick foamboard pieces for the dugout. Glue them into place with white glue, holding them with dressmaking pins until the joints set.

4 Paint the interior of the dugout black. Build the timber posts, beam, and bracing for the entrance from stripwood and glue them into position.

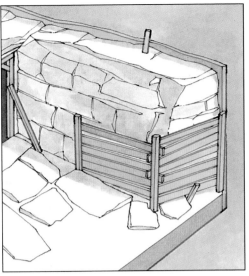

6 Glue some strips of stripwood to form a retaining fence to the right-hand side.

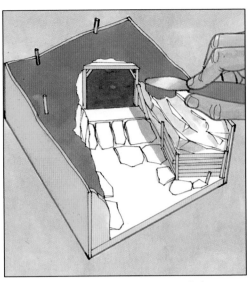

8 Use a palette knife to spread the mixture over the expanded polystyrene. Be careful not to make the finish look as if it had been smoothed with a trowel. Prevent this if necessary by stippling with a damp stiff brush.

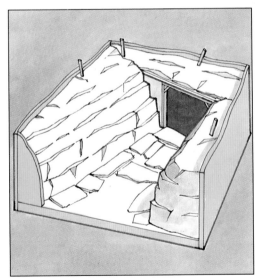

5 Take some pieces of expanded polystyrene from packaging, cut them roughly to shape using a craft knife, and fix into place with a hot glue gun.

7 Prepare a scenic mixture composed of dry household filler powder, black powder paint, brown household latex paint, white glue, and fine sawdust. No water is needed, because the white glue and the latex paint are sufficiently liquid to bind the stiff mixture together.

9 Add sandbags, duckboards, and fence posts to give detail to the dugout entrance.

Wood bridges

In earlier times many bridges were made from wood, because it was easy to obtain in most areas, and easy to work. Even railroad bridges were made from wood, using complex supporting frameworks. A few wood rail bridges remain, but most wood bridges today are only used for foot or light road traffic, or in temporary use on construction sites. There are both wood and plastic construction kits for wooden bridges, but it is not difficult to make your own.

Above Wood trestle bridges can be spectacular, like this tall and wide structure on the HO American Kahoka Falls Railroad layout.

2 Here is a typical example of a light wooden bridge for pedestrians and farm traffic alongside a railroad track. It is made entirely from wood strip to fit the site – crossing a mill stream. The arrangement of planks and supports is straightforward, and the bridge was stained with brown paint that soaked into the wood to give a realistic effect.

1 This light wood bridge was constructed from balsa sheet and strip to carry coalmine "spoil" across a railroad track. The upright support came from a plastic footbridge kit, but the deck and tippler house are of balsa sheet scored to depict wooden planks.

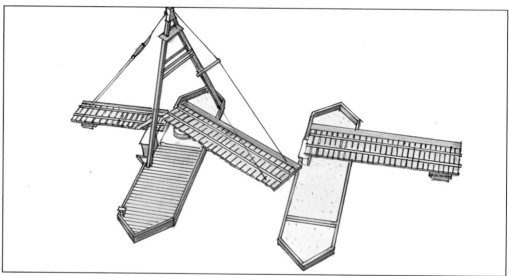

3 An unusual wood bridge, of the type used in the early days of the railroad to span a river and swing back to let boats through. Its construction, of stripwood and balsa sheet, is clear from the illustration. Thick wood strip and wire was used for the swinging supports. On a working model layout, the decking can be glued rigidly in place to allow trains to pass over it.

4 The most famous wood bridge is the trestle bridge, once common for carrying trains, though most have now been replaced by modern descendants. This example is sold as a plastic kit for assembly in large scale, but smaller kits are available, or you can make your own.

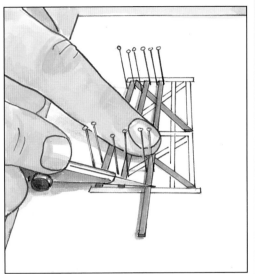

6 Make the bents as follows. Place your drawing on a cork tile, cover it with wax paper, and glue wood strip, cut to length, over the pattern. Use pins to hold the parts in place while the glue sets.

5 The uprights of a trestle bridge are known as bents, and they are made to suit the individual site. Measure the depth to be bridged, and draw your own patterns for the bents, like the ones shown here, to the size you need.

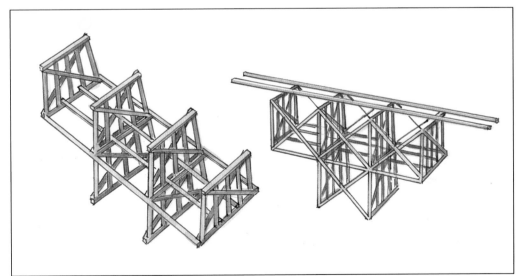

7 Construct as many bents of different depths as you need to span the width and height. Support them with horizontal bracing, and diagonal bracing where necessary, made from wood strip and glued on. Finally add a wooden deck for the track and fit the bridge in the gap.

Stone and steel bridges

Bridges make dramatic additions to any scenic setting, whether on a big railroad layout or a diorama. They also increase authenticity because they emphasize the fact that the land contours are fully modeled, and that therefore a means is needed – as in real life – to get a level highway or railroad across the terrain. There are many construction kits for bridges available, mostly plastic. Bearing in mind that a certain precision and strength is needed on a model railroad if trains are to cross, it is usually best to rely on a kit, but bridges can be built from model materials, as shown here. Cardboard or plastic parts are also available from which bridges can be constructed. Even if you build from a kit, however, you will need to add realistic supports and other details.

Checklist
Materials
Suitable construction kit, or balsa wood/plywood, Cardboard or wood strip, Plastic strip, Brick or stone paper or brick or stone embossed cardboard

Right A bridge can be a stunning addition to any railroad layout or diorama. This is truest in mountain terrain, where a bridge can emphasize the wild and rocky nature of the scenery.

1 This bridge was made from a plastic kit, but the stone abutments to support it were constructed from wooden blocks covered in brick-finish cardboard, and recessed to take the bridge and track bed, as shown.

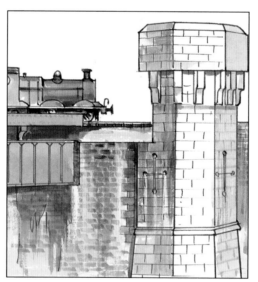

2 An important touch of detail on any bridge model is to add the extensive rain and water dribbles and discoloration that inevitably runs down the sides of the abutments. Do this with diluted water-based paints, such as acrylics, in browns, grays, whites, and blacks.

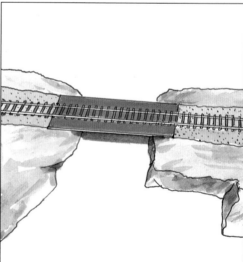

3 You can make a rail bridge that carries weight simply by carrying the plywood track base all the way across the gap, held by the baseboard supports, and building up the bridge pieces around it. Here is the bare trackboard, carrying the track and ballast but not yet detailed.

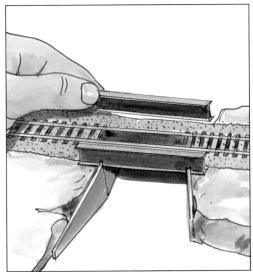

4 The bridge shown is completed by cementing in plate girder sides made from plastic strip, and using embossed cardboard brick sheet cut to shape for the abutments. The sheet was simply glued to the terrain scenery and does not carry any weight.

5 Even if there is no room for a valley on your layout, you can still fit an imposing bridge on a mountainside where the train crosses a ravine to traverse a rocky ledge. This bridge and its pier and abutments are all kit-built, but set up against a cliff face.

Tram tracks

Above Regular model railroad track has been adapted to create tram tracks.

Tram and railroad track set into a road can form an entire layout – in a trolley system for example – or be part of a scenic setting, such as a wharf. Specialized tram track is available from some manufacturers, but is often relatively expensive, and not always suitable. In this project, regular model railroad track is adapted using simple materials and tools to give effective, functioning results.

Checklist

Materials

Railroad track laid on baseboard, 60 thou (1.5mm) thick styrene sheet, ⅛in (3mm) thick cork tiles or similar, Modeling clay, White glue, 1in (25mm) glue brush, H or 2H pencil, Cutting mat, Craft knife, Metal straight-edge

1 After wiring and testing the previously laid railroad track, fill the space between the rails with modeling clay. Use your thumb and fingers to insert clay up to the level of the top of the rail, pushing it well down between the ties. A run of 1ft or 2ft (30–60cm) is a convenient amount to do at a time.

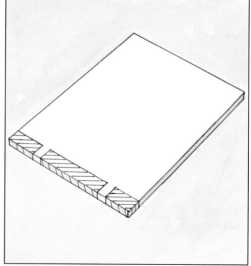

2 Use a small piece of sheet styrene to form a tool for scooping out the necessary groove on the inside of each rail. The track gauge will depend upon the scale and gauge that you are working in. The depth and width must be great enough for the wheel flanges in use; the maximum depth will be to the top of the rail fixings.

3 Drag the tool along the top of the rail surface, as shown, while the modeling clay is still wet. Scrape surplus clay off for reuse.

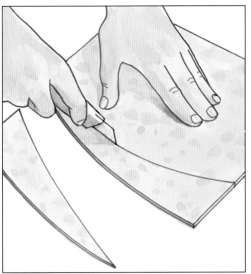

5 Build up the space between the tracks in a material of suitable thickness. This must reach higher than the ties but below the top of the rail. For HO gauge code 100 rail, you can achieve approximately $\frac{1}{32}$in (1mm) below the rail top with $\frac{1}{8}$in (3mm) thick cork tiles sold for home decorating. Cut them with a craft knife into suitable shapes, getting as close as possible to the edge of the ties.

7 Fill the space between the outside of the rails and the edge of the cork with modeling clay. Scrape off the excess level with the top of the cork before the clay dries.

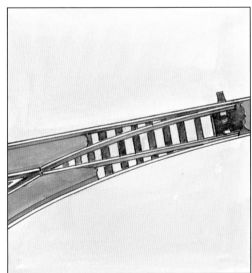

4 Take great care to leave a clear path for the wheel flanges through the switch and check rails. If part of the switch blades of the point is designed not to move, follow the same procedure as before. Where the blades do move, apply the clay very carefully between the ties, but not above them. Check the functioning of the blades before the clay dries.

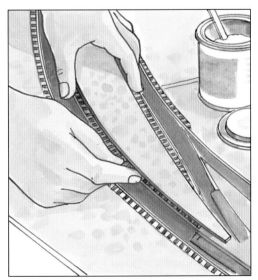

6 Glue the pieces of cork into place with white glue. Be careful to allow space at the side of the track for the movement of the tie bar.

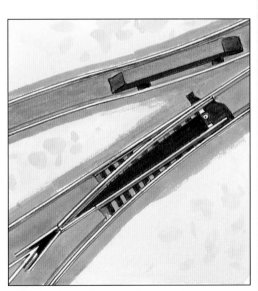

8 At the points, fill the area between the switch blades with suitably sized pieces of styrene sheet. Cut these very carefully to avoid obstructing the passage of the wheel flanges. Remember to calculate the clearance for both settings of the blades.

Ruins

An interesting addition to any layout or diorama is a ruined building, which gives good scope for attractive scenic work and cameo displays of figures. It also tends to catch the eye just as ruins do in real life. Mostly we associate the word "ruin" with old castles and historical houses, but in modeling you can define the term in its widest sense, because a spectacular effect can be obtained from a demolition scene, especially as there are now many fine models of suitable construction plant and workmen figures.

You can buy construction kits for ruined castles and houses, but it is possible to make your own ruins to suit any site by modifying or "distressing" existing parts. Some possible variations are shown here.

Checklist

Materials
Suitable construction kits or odd kit parts or balsa wood remnants, Modeling tools, Selection of paints (mainly grays, white, black, brown, earth colors)

Above An unusual, but once fairly widespread treatment for decaying properties, is to shore them up with heavy wooden baulks to stop them from collapsing. This is very eye-catching in model form, and easy to do with stripwood. In abandoned properties, windows and doors are generally boarded over – simple enough with balsa strips.

1 A commonly seen ruin is a building under demolition, and this can make an effective model. This site features an ordinary house construction kit with the walls modified by sawing and all the roof and window parts omitted. The rubble effect is achieved by crumbling half-set modeling plaster.

2 The extreme opposite, although visually similar to a ruin, is a house under construction. Depict this by sawing suitably sized segments from model building walls, or by covering balsa sheet with brick paper. The door and window frames can come from kits or be constructed from thin stripwood.

3 This is how ruined or partly built walls can be made. Cut a jagged outline in brick (or stone) paper, and glue the paper to balsa sheet. Cut around the outline when the glue is set. Paint the exposed edges in stone or brick color.

4 An alternative is to cut out plastic molded brick (or stone) walling in a similar way, using a very sharp craft knife (with a new blade), or a razor saw – or a combination of both.

Above A ruined castle as most people visualize it is superbly modeled in HO scale, set on a craggy hilltop. Note the moss and grass on the tops of the walls, and trees growing inside the walls – just like the real thing.

5 When modeling a wrecked house or similar structure, you can add a touch or distinction by including the traces of wallpaper, plaster, and the remains of fittings. Draw them on paper and glue them inside the damaged walls. Window frames, with or without "glass," are optional.

Landscape

Living in and among buildings of various types, as most modern people do, we are acutely aware of the significant details of architecture. The same cannot be said of landscape, and relatively simple techniques can often produce results that are widely accepted as representing nature without the level of detail that would be necessary in a model building.

The time needed to construct, say, a 2ft (60cm) run of topography can be reckoned in hours, whereas a similar length of buildings might take weeks, or even months. The human eye and mind can be fairly easily persuaded to accept a model landscape as an accurate represent-ation: when modeling rocks, for example, unless the viewer is a professional geologist, all that is needed is a suitable shape that has texture and broken color.

In all modelmaking the builder engages in a kind of theater, and therefore theatrical techniques apply. The "audience" must be convinced by illusion, because nature itself displays its work on a scale far too large to be included in most models. There must be selective compression of size and space, along with careful analysis to recognize and incorporate the essential dramatic elements. Successfully done, this can create a persuasive impression, or be ex-ploited to produce a deliberately exaggerated "caricature."

Above The finished scenic shell is used here to provide a suitable background for a 1:43 vehicle and figures.

Basic scenic shell

This project shows the construction of a basic scenic shell from inexpensive everyday materials. Only the simplest of tools are needed. The shell is lightweight and easy to modify. Small modules can be built on a chipboard base, with profile boards of scrap plywood at the back and ends. The shell is formed from a mesh of strips cut from a cereal carton and covered with newspaper.

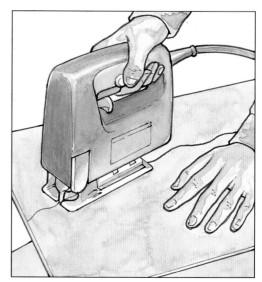

1 Cut a profile board in ¼in (6mm) plywood. Here, an offcut is shaped with a power jig saw, but this could be done by hand using a coping saw.

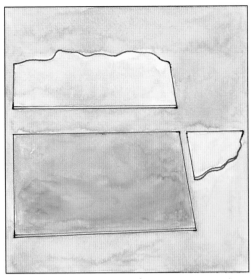

2 The components after cutting consist of two ¼in (6mm) profile boards and a base of ½in (12mm) chipboard.

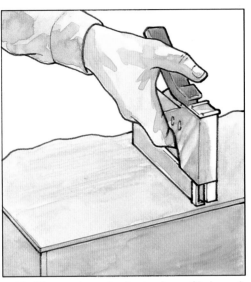

4 Glue and staple the back profile board at right angles to the edge of the base. Use a heavy-duty staple gun or tacker to fire ⅝in (14mm) long pins through the profile board into the base.

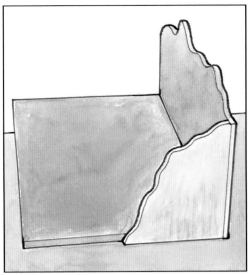

6 Add the end profile at right angles to the back board to complete assembly of one end of the scenic module. Ordinarily, another profile board would be fitted at the other end.

3 Coat the back edge of the chipboard base with white glue.

5 Alternatively, regular carpentry nails can be driven in with a hammer.

7 Cut strips of cardboard about ¾in (15–20mm) wide from a cereal carton or other packaging. Produce a good supply of these, cut as long as possible, using a metal ruler, knife, and cutting mat.

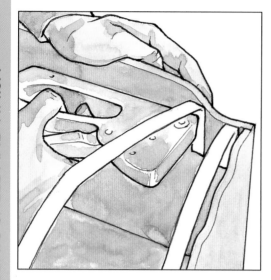

8 Begin fixing the strips to the back board and the base, parallel with the end profile board. Use a staple gun for speed, or a hot glue gun.

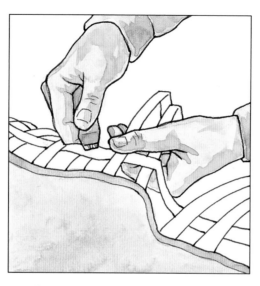

10 Begin interweaving a second set of strips at right angles to the first. Tack the strips together using staple pliers – a hot glue gun could be used instead.

12 When you have built up a complete mesh, assemble the materials and equipment for the next step: pieces of newspaper torn into shapes approximately 1½in (30–40mm) square, dilute white glue, a flat brush, and an old plate.

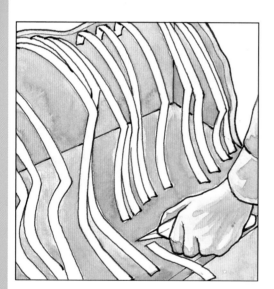

9 Leave a gap of around ¾–1in (20–25mm) between each strip, and when you reach the end of the module trim off the excess from the base. The strips roughly follow the line of the end profile board and the intended final appearance of the topography being modeled.

11 The second woven strip should be about ¾–1in (20–25mm) from the first. Repeat, following the line of the back board.

13 Soak the newspaper pieces in the diluted glue. Enough squares to cover the plate – say, 9 or 10 – can be treated at a time.

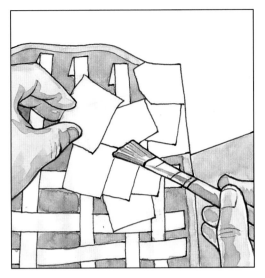

14 Apply the pieces to the mesh of cardboard strips, using the brush and more dilute glue to fix them in place.

16 The aim is to cover the entire cardboard mesh with two layers of newspaper. At this stage the structure will lack strength because the surface is soggy. Once complete, it must be set aside to dry. It will then gain the necessary strength and tension to serve as the basic shell for the topography.

18 Glue small strips of mounting board along the center of the road, with white glue or a hot glue gun. These will have the effect of introducing a camber to the road surface.

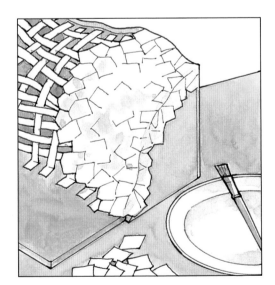

15 At the end of the module, glue the squares around the corners onto the profile boards.

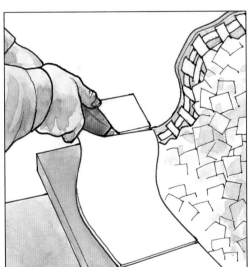

17 Cut a piece of mat board to represent a road. This will run at the foot of the rock face on the finished module. In this case, scrap pieces are used, making it necessary to include a join. This will not be evident when the module is completed.

19 Fix the road into position using a staple gun. You could do this with a hot glue gun, or apply white glue and weight the piece down until the adhesive sets.

Basic scenic finish

A combination of household filler, regular latex paint, and sawdust provides a scenic shell covering that you can treat to produce attractive settings for the display of many different structures, figures, or vehicles. Paint the coating using texture and broken color to portray rocks, or treat it with a commercial finish to represent grass, foliage, and other features.

Checklist

Materials

Powder filler for household repairs, Black powder paint, Latex paint (brown, black, white), Sawdust, Commercial finishes (ground foam, dark green and medium green; small mineral chippings), Newspaper, Screw-top jars, 1in (25mm) flat brush, Water, White glue, Damp cloth, Pipette, Old plate, Airbrush or plant spray bottle, Hair dryer (optional)

2 Coat the area of the paper shell that will become the rock face with undiluted white glue, and sprinkle the filler mixture onto it through a small kitchen sieve.

4 Apply the same filler mixture in an identical way to the road surface and the rest of the base and leave to dry. Sand the road surface and brush or shake off any loose coating and collect it for future use. This is especially easy with modules that can be turned upside down.

1 Mix a small quantity of the powder filler used for household repairs with black powder paint. This is to prevent the pale color of the filler showing through if cracking subsequently occurs. Black is used in this case because the rock is to be gray. The exact proportions of the mixture do not matter provided the result is a mid- to dark gray.

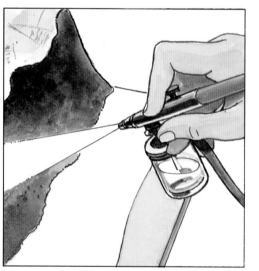

3 Spray water onto the coating so that it soaks through and bonds the covering to the shell. The water can be most easily controlled with an airbrush, but a spray bottle designed for misting house plants also works well. The filler must be thoroughly and evenly wet but not sodden.

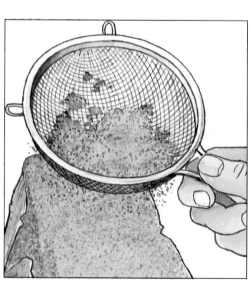

5 Paint patches of thick brown latex (in any shade suitable for soil) onto the area that will be grass at the top of the rock face. Sprinkle each patch with fine sawdust and press it down. This stage is not essential, but it contributes texture and gives a "key" to the section that will be grassed. Some areas of the roadside are similarly treated.

6 Paint the rock face using the dry brush technique. For this module, black, white, and the previously used brown shades of latex paint are all that is needed. Apply a darkish gray first, then progressively lighter layers, one with a touch of brown, and finally a very pale gray.

8 Apply commercially produced ground foam material for the grass. This is available in various colors. Here, a random mix of dark and medium green was chosen. Give the areas previously treated with sawdust (step 5) another coat of brown latex paint. As before, paint small patches at a time, sprinkle on the ground foam, and press it down on the wet paint.

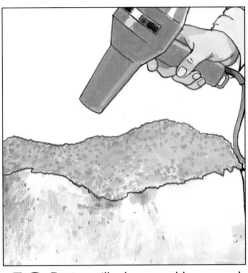

10 Drying will take several hours, and the process can be speeded with a hair dryer.

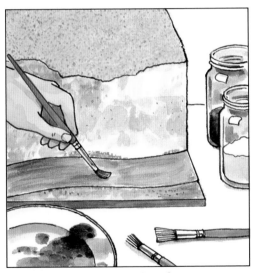

7 Dry brush the road surface in a similar way, using shades of gray and aiming for a darker appearance than that of the rock face.

9 Brush off any loose ground foam and collect it for future use. Then fix the grassed area firmly by soaking it with a 50/50 mixture of white glue and water to which a small amount of dishwashing detergent has been added: this breaks the surface tension and ensures that the liquid disperses throughout the foam. Tilt the module to prevent the diluted glue from running down the rock face. If this happens, mop it immediately with a slightly damp cloth.

11 Add detail to the roadside with ground foam grass, and pieces of suitably colored stone chippings (also sold for scenic dressing), dropped onto patches of paint or white glue. Apply a finishing touch by using a dry pipette to puff some of the remaining filler and powder paint mixture around the roadside.

Modeling rock

Above The finished rockwork after meticulous painting.

This project shows the modeling of a substantial rock outcrop. Use expanded polystyrene to form the basic shape. Then apply modeling clay, and carefully carve and paint it to represent the rock strata.

Checklist

Materials

½in (12mm) thick chipboard, ¼in (6mm) plywood, Expanded polystyrene packaging or tiles, Small section stripwood, Modeling clay, Torn newspaper, White glue, Cyanoacrylate glue, Scenic dressing (long bristles for grass), Acrylic paints, Enamel paints, H or 2H pencil, 1in (25mm) glue brush, Damp cloth, Fine sandpaper, Hot glue gun, Craft knife with snap-off blade, X-Acto handle and blade, Small hammer and nails or heavy-duty staple gun, Power jig saw, Hair dryer (optional)

1 Make a supporting structure from a piece of chipboard and two short lengths of plywood. Our components were left over from household use. Cut the chipboard roughly to shape with a power jig saw, and pin and glue the plywood pieces to it to form a corner as shown.

2 The inner core will be boxed off and left hollow. To do this, fix two wooden strips to the base with white glue, and pin with a staple gun or hammer.

3 Add a vertical panel of scrap plywood, and another horizontal piece above. Pin and glue the pieces into place.

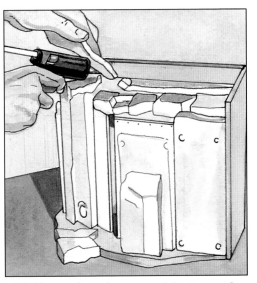

5 Using a hot glue gun, stick pieces of expanded polystyrene packaging onto the unit. Expanded polystyrene tiles can be utilized instead.

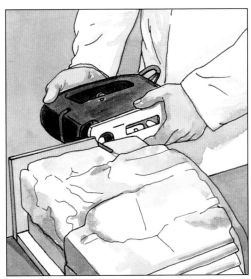

7 Placing the unit first on one side and then on another, cut the plywood and chipboard pieces back to the shape of the polystyrene, using a power jig saw.

4 Fit a second vertical piece of plywood in the same way. It is not necessary to close the box completely.

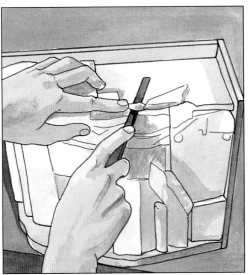

6 Trim the polystyrene to shape with a long, smooth-edged craft knife blade (a previously unused "snap-off" type is ideal). Do not use a blade with a serrated edge, since this greatly increases the amount of debris created.

8 Check the unit for overall shape. It was deliberately designed to have two flat sides, and a protruding piece on the exposed corner. Sand the base, rear, and side flat to improve the presentation.

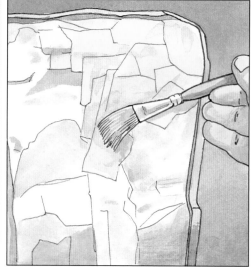

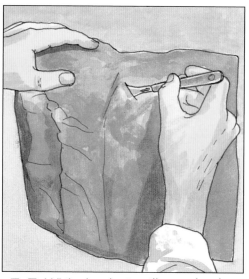

9 Stick small pieces of torn newspaper all over the polystyrene with diluted white glue to unify the surface of the unit. Allow to dry overnight or speed dry with a hair dryer.

11 While the clay is still wet, sketch the basic rock strata into it with an X-Acto knife.

13 Allow the modeling clay to dry overnight and carve additional strata details with the X-Acto knife.

10 When the newspaper is completely dry, apply terracotta-colored modeling clay to create the rock surface. Smooth the clay on by hand and finish with a wet finger.

12 Stipple the wet clay on the top (horizontal) surface of the unit, using a stiff paintbrush. This will create a "key" for an area of thin soil, where a small amount of vegetation will later be modeled.

14 Paint the entire unit with a basic brown wash of acrylic paint.

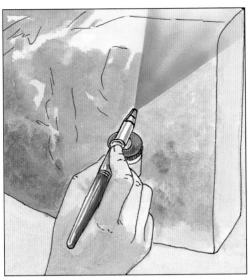

15 Airbrush the unit with acrylic paint in various red browns. Then dry brush it with enamel paint to provide highlights.

16 Add some vegetation to the top horizontal surface. This takes the form of scrubby grass, represented by commercial scenic material of the bristle type. Fix it down with cyanoacrylate glue, and mist it with an airbrush to reduce the shine.

Above The use of expanded polystyrene to build the walls of this rock cutting enabled the basic form to be produced very quickly. Then it was covered in modeling clay, imprinted with pieces of real rock, painted, and scenic dressing was applied to the top surfaces.

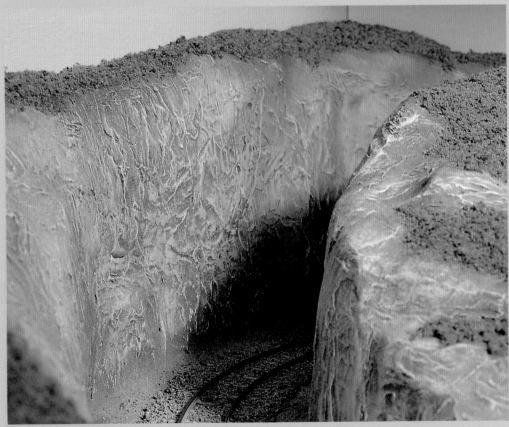

Above This rock face has been modeled using the expanded polystyrene and modeling clay technique. It is, in fact, a hollow scenic feature, which would allow for features such as a railroad tunnel to be modeled into it if desired.

Water

There are many ways of depicting water in miniature and the easiest methods are shown here. Sometimes real water is used, especially in large-scale settings, and there are some plastic kits of watermills and fountains where water is moved in a closed circuit by a small electric pump built into the model. These are special cases, however, and generally actual water is too messy and impractical. Moreover, in small scales it often looks unrealistic because it is too viscous! Therefore, the artificial ways of representing it are usually the best.

The first two of the methods shown here are by far the simplest, and the best for beginners.

Checklist

Materials

Gloss paints (blues, greens, black, white, etc.), Assorted glues, Hardboard or styrene sheet, Clear acrylic gloss varnish, X-Acto knife, Modeling plaster, Level, Clear casting resin, Wide soft paintbrush, Clear plastic sprue, Candle

Above This water looks so wet you feel you could dip your fingers in it! Note the realistic reflections, disturbed water around the wooden piles, and a seaweed line on the jetty to suggest tidal variation. This effect is achieved with clear varnish and paint.

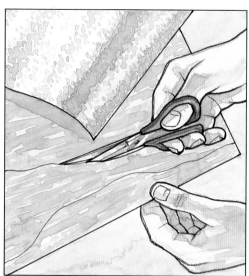

1 One of the easiest methods is to use the imitation "water" made in rolls or sheets by several of the well-known producers of structure and scenic kits. This "water" is usually thin opaque tinted blue plastic with a rippled surface, which can be cut to shape with a model knife or scissors. Some manufacturers supply a transparent rippled sheet along with blue or blue-green cardboard to use underneath it for added "depth."

2 Water material is most suitable for fast-moving streams or rivers, as in this example. It is important to keep the sheet completely horizontal to avoid an uphill effect. Form a dam by putting a ridge of cardboard beneath the sheet and lightly apply white gloss paint to depict the disturbed water. Miniature ducks (left) can also be painted in with white. Pin or glue the water sheet at its edges, and cover to width with the river banks afterward.

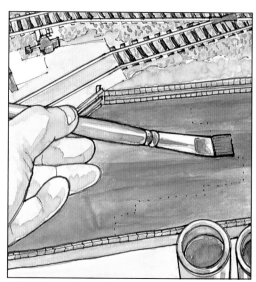

3 A simple way to depict still water is by painting. Use a smooth surface, such as hardboard or thick styrene sheet and paint over it with gloss blue, blue-black, or greenish-blue to give the desired color. Ensure smooth coverage with no brushmarks, bristles, or dust dried into the surface to ruin the effect. For shallower water near the edge, you could lighten the paint with a touch of white or pale gray.

4 Leave the painted surface overnight to dry hard. Then brush quick-drying acrylic gloss varnish all over it. Do this in a dust-free area if possible (the bathroom is a good place!) to avoid particles drying in the varnish and spoiling the effect. Leave overnight again to dry hard, and repeat the process two or three more times if desired, though the "wet" effect is good after even one coat.

6 The varnish technique is best for still water, such as harbor basins and ponds, but it can also be used as the finishing touch for rough water, such as on a beach or sea-wall scene. Model the waves with regular modeling plaster, and when it is dry, paint it blue or blue-green water color, adding white flecks for the foaming crests. When this is thoroughly dry, brush over with clear gloss varnish as before.

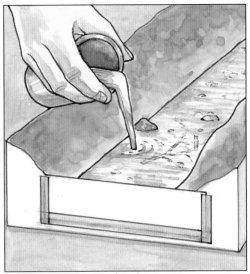

8 Use a level to check that the entire baseboard or diorama is perfectly level. Then pour clear casting resin (mixed according to the manufacturer's instructions) over the pond or river area, and leave it to set hard. A word of caution: the resin will flow until it sets, so it must be level to avoid "uphill water", and any open end must be dammed with styrene or thin plywood to prevent the resin from pouring away. Remove the "dam" when the resin is set.

5 The completed surface has a deep, wet look that gives realistic reflections like these. Cut boats down to waterline level, and trim the legs of any wading figures to give a correct "in the water" effect.

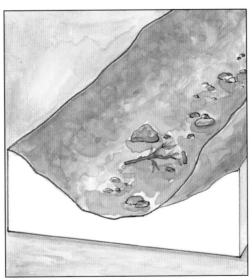

7 This method is ideal for shallow rivers or ponds, where you may want to depict detail below the water surface. Begin by modeling the river or pond bed with plaster, gluing in any rocks, submerged logs, or even old bedsteads! Paint it in full colors and leave to dry.

9 Depict water flowing from a pipe, or a small waterfall, by means of the clear plastic sprue (holding frame) left over from the window parts in a kit. Hold the sprue above a candle flame until the plastic softens, distorts, and sags. Do not let it become discolored by the smoke. Prepare a selection of these, and choose the most suitable shapes for your purposes. Add touches of white gloss paint to suggest flurries of water around the falling plume.

Modeling a tree

Above The completed tree, mounted and displayed on a small scenic base.

This project shows the technique for constructing a fairly large tree. It is most suitable when a limited number of trees are needed – for example, in a small military diorama. The basic structure is built of wire, and some commercially produced scenic materials are added. Once you are familiar with the method, you can make several trees at a time.

Checklist

Materials

Wire, Masking tape, Brown latex paint, Brown (household) latex paint, Various green model paints (enamel or acrylic), Household filler, Foliage fiber, Ground foam, White glue, Spray adhesive, Side cutters, Palette knife, ¼in (6mm) brush for glue, Airbrush

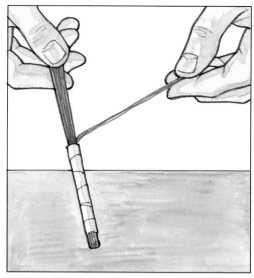

1 Bind a bundle of wire strands with masking tape. Take a batch of strands, bend them to one side, and twist them together for a short distance from the base to make a side branch.

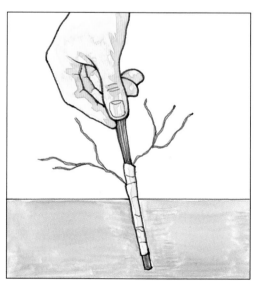

2 Split the strands, bend them outward again, and twist them a little further to form a secondary branch. Bind the trunk with masking tape above the first branch, and produce another side branch in the same way.

3 Continue the process until the basic shape looks like this. Remove any surplus wire with side cutters.

5 Tease out small pieces of commercial foliage fiber, and begin fixing it to the branches with white glue. Build up the overall shape of the tree with more pieces of foliage fiber.

7 Apply spray adhesive to areas of the foliage fiber. Take care to spray in a well ventilated room.

4 Make a mixture of white glue, brown latex paint, and household filler, and spread it over the wire and masking tape with a palette knife to represent bark. Apply the mixture as far up the wire branches as possible, and leave to dry overnight.

6 Spray the foliage fiber with dark brown paint and leave to dry overnight.

8 Sprinkle scenic decoration (sold as ground foam) over the spray adhesive. Do this over a clean sheet of newspaper, so that you can collect the fallen ground foam and reuse it. Spray the foliage carefully in various shades of green.

Trees and bushes

1 Making a tree from a kit. This series provides a soft metal cast trunk and a sheet of realistic foliage. The metal is pliant enough to be varied in shape by bending the branches. From left to right: the cast metal trunk and foliage as supplied; the trunk bent to the desired shape and painted matte bark color, with foliage application started; the rest of the foliage teased out and stuck to the branches, using white glue. Any remaining foliage pieces can be kept for other trees, or used as weeds or bushes.

3 Many modern ready-made trees are of recognizable species, such as these poplars, sold in sets. Here they are "planted" to form a lifelike screen, a good way of introducing a "visual break" on a model railroad layout when trains pass behind the trees partially out of view. This makes a layout seem larger than it is.

In the past miniature trees were a problem. Ready-made trees were either exquisitely detailed and expensive, or cheap but crude and toylike. Many modelers, therefore, chose to make their own – a long task on a large layout that might contain hundreds of trees. Today this has changed. Almost all of the companies that produce the building kits also supply kits of trees or ready-made models of identifiable species. In addition, there are many inexpensive though somewhat nondescript conifers that are ideal where a large number of trees is needed. We show you how the appearance of these can be improved and how to use different trees to create variety within a setting. Your model supplier will carry some or all of these tree kits and ready-made trees.

2 A similar kit provides flexible plastic trunk and branch moldings, which can be bent and twisted to shape. A selection of foliage packs is supplied with these sets to give slightly different textures. Once again, the foliage is glued on to choice with white glue. Note the spigot at the base to facilitate fitting into the ground surface, but bases are also supplied so that they can be free-standing.

4 This view shows how model trees can be "planted." The poplars shown in step 3 were sawn from their free-standing bases, and the plastic trunks were painted with a mixture of matte brown and gray bark color to make them more realistic. Holes are then pierced in the ground surface, and the trunks are inserted.

Checklist

Materials
Flock powder, Ground foam, Foliage packs (from model stores), Twigs or old electric wire for home construction or complete tree kits to choice, Tweezers, Craft knife, Paints, White glue

5 A bank of model trees of different heights and textures can give a most realistic effect. All of these trees were made from tree kits similar to those in steps 1 and 2. In the foreground, some surplus tree foliage was fashioned and glued in place to depict a large bush.

Above Realistic trees can add an attractive atmosphere to any scenic model, such as in this country lumber yard. Although green leaves are most commonly seen, it is possible to obtain spectacular autumn foliage, and some models are now produced with a fall option like the one used here.

6 A particular use for model trees is to disguise scenic "short cuts." This church, from a plastic kit, is actually only half a church, set against the background like a piece of stage scenery. The big trees at each end disguise the joint with the backscene and conceal the fact that the church is not built to full depth.

Above An unusual but very attractive model is this hop plantation, complete with its support poles and rigging, and using a variety of figures and equipment to show harvesting in progress. This would be an interesting scenic addition to any model railroad layout or diorama featuring a brewery. The scale is 1:87.

Earth and vegetation

All diorama and baseboard work needs a basic covering of suitable contours, earth, and vegetation. How much you do depends upon the complexity of the scene you wish to reproduce, and how big it is. To show off a model cart, for example, you may only need a flat grassy base, in which case you can simply cover a plywood sheet with dummy grass and vegetation and place the card on it. However, most scenes need more than that, and it is a good idea to introduce some contours to achieve greater realism.

Some work is easier than others. If you are modeling the area around a station or a farmyard, for instance, the ground may be very low, and only low contours will be needed. Tall hills, mountains, or tunnels, on the other hand, will need a more elaborate support structure in order to build up the contours. Here both extremes of work are shown. In all cases you will need either modeling plaster, which is carried by model stores, or regular domestic filling plaster from a hardware store. Mix the plaster to a thick consistency in an old dish or foil tray, adding some brown or black powder paint. This colors the plaster throughout, so that if any cracks appear with time, they will not show stark white to spoil your scenic illusion.

Above This composite view shows all the stages of building ground, earth, and basic vegetation in a single demonstration setting. From the left: the sub-structure covered in brown paper; coated with a layer of plaster; given a rock and grass finish; with trees and bushes added.

Checklist

Materials

Flock powder or scatter coat in various greens and browns to choice, Modeling or patching plaster, Old stiff paintbrush, Old polystyrene packaging blocks, Polystyrene ceiling tiles, Craft knife with heavy-duty blade, Model knife, White glue, Strips of cardboard from old cereal packets, Scrim or gauze or old sacking, Small tacks or pins, Masking tape

1 For low heights and simple settings, cut polystyrene tiles or packaging into shapes and layer them to make hills and cuts for railroad tracks. Use white glue or pins to hold the layers together. Spread old newspaper beneath the work to catch the many plastic granules that will be generated.

2 This layered cut was covered with model plaster to create an earth and rock effect, and coated with white glue. Flock powder is now shaken over the glue through an old tea strainer to depict the grass surface.

3 Larger areas need more complex treatment. To build this hill, a core of old polystyrene packaging material was roughly carved to shape, and extended with strips of cardboard cut from cereal packets, interwoven to create the shape of the slope. Use pins and white glue to keep everything together.

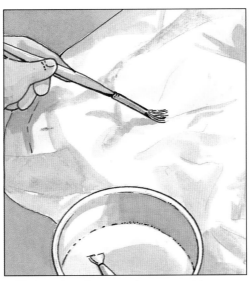

5 Mix the plaster, coloring it with powder paint. Use a paintbrush to apply it in a thin layer over the entire surface. When dry, apply one or more additional layers of plaster to form a stiff shell. The application in thin layers speeds drying; thick layers can crack or crumble.

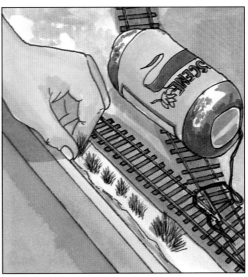

7 For economy, or greater variation, cut short lengths of green garden twine, tease them out with your fingers, and stick the resulting clumps to the ground surface. Several clumps can be built into a bush. Stick the clumps down with white glue, or pierce holes in the plaster with a small screwdriver, pour in the glue, and insert the clumps.

4 Cover the assembly with scrim, old gauze, sacking, or crumpled brown wrapping paper. Use glue or masking tape to hold it lightly in place.

6 The completed hillside can be painted grass green, earth brown, or rocky gray, depending upon the terrain you wish to depict. Then paint on a layer of thinned white glue, and sprinkle with flock powder as in step 2.

8 A completed hillside, with the grass and vegetation in place, and a building added. Plaster was built up around the base of the house, so that it looks as though it is built into the ground, not just placed on top of it.

Figures and animals

Figures give a sense of scale to many types of model, and are often essential to realism. Details such as doors and windows can give a clear indication of the size of model buildings, but model rocks, water, and vegetation can be used successfully in more than one scale.

Figures are often central to the interests of military modelers, and uniforms are a crucial element — sometimes virtually the subject of the model. Figures are also important to model railroaders, but for them the suitability of action poses is a significant factor.

Some military modelers seek to show a specific moment — for example, in a battle — and therefore

use an approach similar to a snapshot that "freezes" an instant. Model railroaders, however, are concerned with locomotives that actually move trains along the track. Their models operate, whereas most figures currently do not. This is true whatever the scale being used, and does impose certain requirements.

Model railroad figures are best portrayed in non-action poses. Resist the temptation to represent a figure in the action of flagging a train out of a yard, since however realistic this looks when the train is leaving, the same figure interminably frozen in that pose long after the departure will inevitably seem pointless and toylike. Far better to choose a more

reflective pose: the woodsman leaning on his axe contemplating the mighty redwood will look fine, but with arms above his head, frozen in mid-swing, he will look ridiculous, and give the scene the tension of awaiting a blow that never falls.

Large-scale scratchbuilt figure

The most satisfying model is the one that you design and build yourself. Unlimited by kits and ready-made components, you can let your imagination work on producing a unique item. All that you need is research information, along with suitable materials and tools – and your own enthusiasm. The greatest challenge lies in the design process: a successful result depends upon careful planning and preparation.

Checklist

Materials

Research materials, Sketch of armature, ⅛in (3mm) square-section wire, Wooden base, Styrene sheet in various thicknesses, Two-part epoxy putty, Two-part epoxy glue, Suitable paints, Airbrush, Small paintbrushes, Ruler, H or 2H pencil, Cutting mat, Try square, X-Acto handle and blades, Metal straight-edge, Thin brass strip, Saucepan, Water

Above The finished Samurai. The precise painting needed to bring out all the detail took many hours.

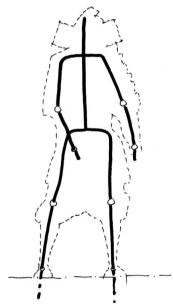

1 After studying suitable research material, make a full-size sketch of the armature wire shape for a 4½in (120mm) high figure.

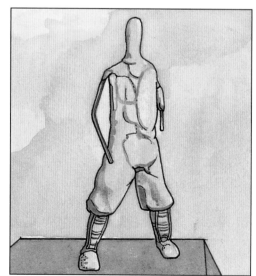

2 Use ⅛in (3mm) square-section armature wire to build up the basic pose of the figure. The wire for the legs must be long enough to push into holes in a suitable base that will act as a stand and handling unit during the construction. Cover the wire frame with epoxy putty and begin shaping the figure. Some aspects can be modeled before the putty sets, and others when it is solid and able to be carved.

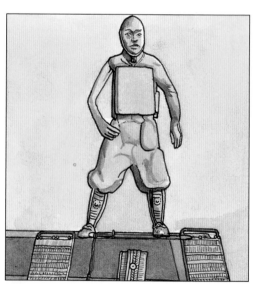

3 Build the flat pieces of regalia and armor out of epoxy putty on suitably sized pieces of thin styrene. Shape the body to receive the flat armor: here, the chest section is ready, and the right arm will be modeled later.

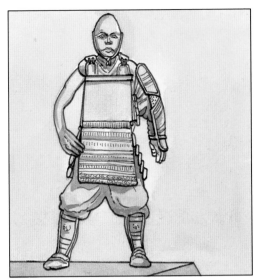

4 Fit the pieces of armor into place, and model the details of the left arm.

6 The model is intended to be viewed from all angles, so the detailing of the armor pieces and clothes continues on the rear of the figure.

Small scratchbuilt figure

Building your own small figures gives greater flexibility and ensures that they perfectly complement your scene. This figure is intended for a World War I trench scene and adapts the method used for the large-scale figure to a 1:32 scale. Only four components are needed: a commercial head, a wire frame, masking tape, and some two-part epoxy putty.

Checklist

Materials
Whitemetal head, 40 thou (1mm) diameter brass wire, Cyanoacrylate glue, Masking tape, Side cutters, Pliers, Miniature sculpting tools, Two-part epoxy putty

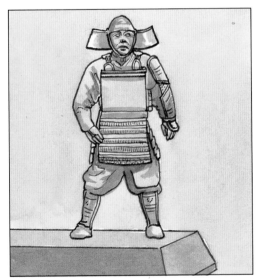

5 Build up the right arm and form the helmet. The complex shape of the headgear is achieved by taping a thin sheet of styrene to a thicker strip of brass that is bent and cut to shape. Mold the styrene to the shape of the brass by placing the two in boiling water. After cooling, trim the edge to shape. The brass is then discarded.

7 Spray the completed figure with a coat of gray or brown paint. This unifies the entire piece before the final painting. It also acts as a "witness coat," so that any imperfections of surface detail and texture show up, and can be remedied before proceeding further.

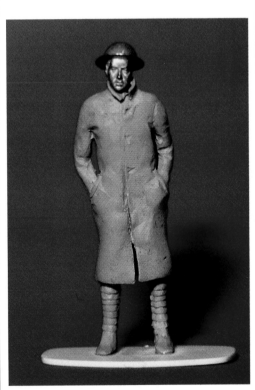

Above The complete model before painting.

1 Make a frame from 40 thou (1mm) diameter brass wire. Do this in two parts: the right arm, side of body, and leg; and then the left. Use cyanoacrylate glue to attach the two halves and a commercial whitemetal head – these are sold in packs and have a fixing spigot at the base of the neck. Bind the body with masking tape while the glue sets.

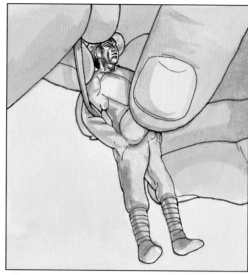

3 Continue building the figure with the putty and modeling the pose and clothes. Some of the modeling is done with suitable tools after the putty has set. Sculpt folds in the clothing at body joints with a miniature carving tool.

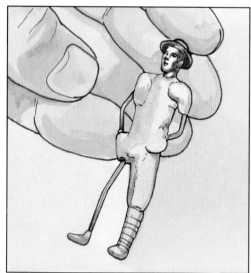

2 Bend the wire limbs into a realistic pose at the shoulders, elbows, hips, and knees. Leaving the masking tape in place, begin building up the body with two-part epoxy putty applied in small blobs. Start detailed shaping with a small sculpting tool before the putty sets.

4 To portray the figure's military greatcoat, roll some epoxy putty into a flat sheet before application.

Kit-built figure

Standard figures are available from model-making suppliers in various materials in the form of kits for assembly. This project shows the assembly of one such figure, designed to portray a US Marine, following the manufacturer's instructions. The scale is 1:32.

Checklist
Materials
Plastic kit, Styrene solvent, X-Acto handle and blade

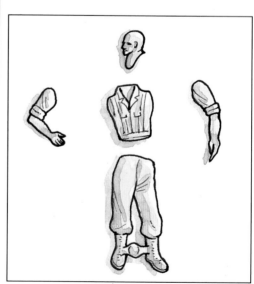

1 This is a plastic figure in which the body comes in parts. Remove these from the sprue (the plastic structure on which they are mounted).

Above The completed kit figure.

4 Fix the equipment bags at the back.

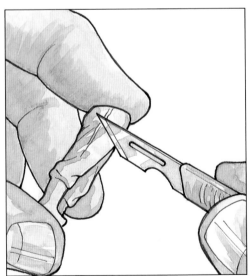

2 Carefully scrape away the surplus plastic (the flash) along the line of the mold join using a sharp blade.

3 Glue the torso to the legs section with styrene solvent. Fix the head in the same way. Begin to add the detail parts of the kit: the bayonet and belt pouches.

5 Glue the arms into place and fit the helmet.

Simple kit figure conversion

Above The completed figure, after assembly and modification.

The modeled plastic US Marine figure on the preceding pages can easily be changed into a civilian workman. All you need to do to effect this transformation is to remove some unwanted plastic and add some modeling in two-part epoxy putty. The pose is not modified.

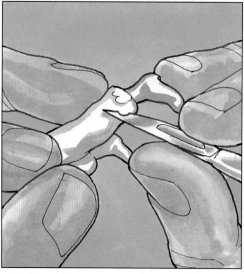

1 Carefully pare away the bunching of the trousers over the boots with a sharp X-Acto blade.

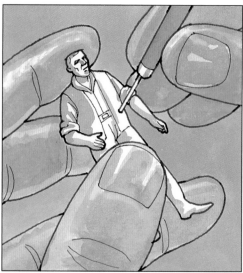

3 Apply two-part epoxy putty to the torso to form a vest, and model it with a suitable tool before it dries.

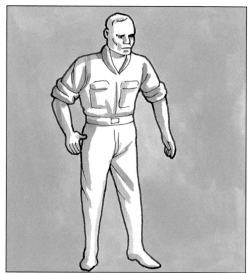

2 Remove the ammunition belts from the torso in the same way, including those at the back, as shown here. Then assemble the basic figure, using styrene solvent.

4 Use more epoxy putty to extend the trousers down to the shoes, and to form a beret.

Mounted figure

This project shows how to modify a mounted plastic figure and horse. The 2¼in (54mm) figure – similar in scale to 1:32 – originated as a kit for an 1815 British lifeguard. It is remodeled to portray a North American trapper of the late 19th century.

Checklist

Materials

Plastic kit, Styrene sheet, Styrene solvent, Two-part epoxy putty, Toilet tissue, Dilute white glue, Cyanoacrylate glue, X-Acto handle and blade, Miniature sculpting tools

Above The complete mounted figure before painting.

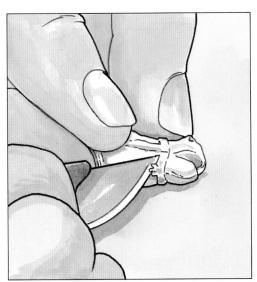

1 Remove the elaborate details of the horse's bridle with a sharp, pointed X-Acto blade.

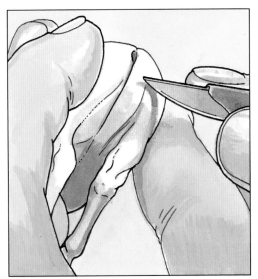

2 Most of the parts of the horse are glued together with solvent. Any flash left along the mold lines should be removed by gently scraping away with the knife.

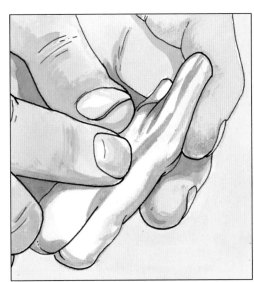

3 Smooth two-part epoxy putty into any gaps between body parts, with the help of a dampened finger.

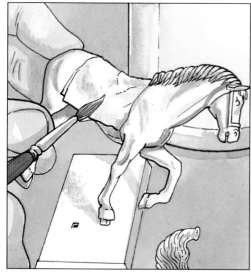

4 With the horse completely assembled, now start work on the saddle cloth. Make the first layer from toilet tissue, carefully cut to size, then stiffened and fixed by soaking in dilute white glue.

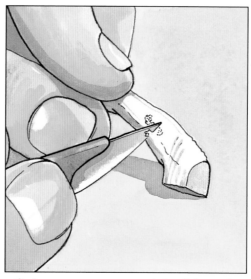

6 Scrape away unwanted detail from the human figure with a sharp, pointed blade.

8 Assemble the modified figure, and add a disk of styrene sheet to the flattened top of the head. The rest of the figure is unadorned, although the pose remains appropriate for a rider seated on a horse.

5 Add a second layer of tissue in the same way, over the first.

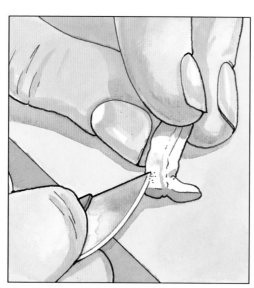

7 Pare away the elaborate military spurs.

9 Add new detail, including a longer coat, the top of the hat and a full beard, using two-part epoxy putty. Detail the rear of the coat with a strip of putty to show that it is made of animal skin. The rolled blanket comes from the original kit. At this stage, the figure is posed on the horse but not fixed.

10 Add the sheepskin saddle built from epoxy putty, and the firearm, modified from the original kit.

Mounted American Indian

Above The completed model ready for painting.

11 Apply additional skins across the rear of the saddle. Create the surface detail on these by careful use of miniature sculpting tools before the putty sets hard. Glue the figure to the horse with cyanoacrylate.

The preceding project modified a mounted plastic figure and horse. Here, the figure is largely built from scratch, and because it is only lightly clothed, it needs considerable body modeling and sculpting. This is therefore a challenging figure modeling project. The scale is 1:32.

Checklist

Materials
Parts from a plastic kit, 40 thou and 30 thou brass wire, Very thin styrene sheet, Two-part epoxy putty, Cyanoacrylate glue, Miniature sculpting tools

1 The horse for this model was carefully selected from those commercially available. A fairly small example was needed to represent the ponies used by the American Indians. The horse came from a plastic kit, so it was shaved of unnecessary bridles and tack, and the flash lines were scraped off the molding.

2 Build an armature from 40 thou brass wire for the basic body. This is in three parts: the right-hand side of the body; the left-hand side (each incorporating the forearms and feet); and a central piece forming the spine, which is fixed to the head, and into the rump of the horse. Join the pieces with glue and bind a small piece of masking tape around the body. Bend the figure to a seated pose. The forearms, feet, and head come from a plastic figure supplied in parts.

4 Working from the thighs, develop the body with the putty, blending into the plastic feet and up into the buttocks and waist.

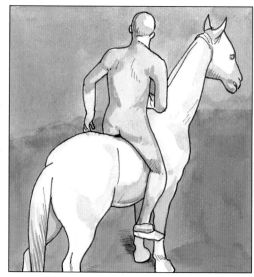

6 Pay just as much attention to the back of the figure as the front. Here, careful modeling of the shoulders can be seen.

3 At this stage it is essential to check the pose from all angles and to make any modifications necessary so that it looks right from every viewpoint. Use two-part epoxy putty to begin building the figure. Model the thighs first.

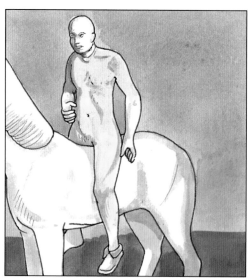

5 Continue upward to the chest and arms, blending the putty into the plastic forearm and head sections. Remodel the shoes of the original plastic feet into moccasins.

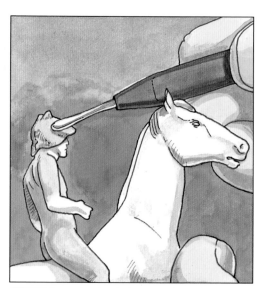

7 When the body is complete, leave the putty to dry hard overnight. Then apply more of the material to the head.

8 Before this begins to dry, sculpt it with a suitably sized modeling tool to form the wolfskin headdress.

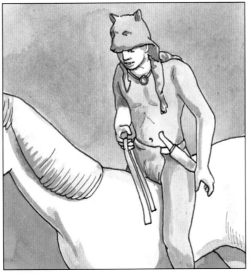

10 Put in ornamental and other details: thin styrene straps in the right hand for the shield; a knife from the spares box (this could be cut from styrene); and the scabbard, necklace, and braided hair in epoxy putty.

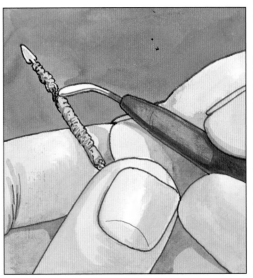

12 Make the lance by applying epoxy putty to a length of 30 thou brass wire, using a modeling tool.

9 Add a belt of very thin styrene strip and a loincloth formed from more epoxy putty.

11 Extend the wolfskin headdress down the back of the figure with epoxy putty, etched with a finely pointed modeling tool.

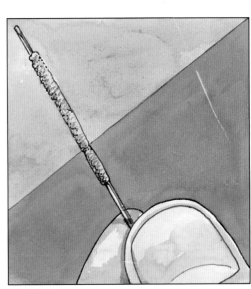

13 Detail the putty before it sets to represent bindings made of buffalo hide.

Painting figures

Various types of paints can be used to paint figures, including enamels, acrylics, and artist's oils. The choice is largely a matter of personal preference, and you will discover by trial and experimentation the medium that suits you best. Enamel paints are the easiest to use for relatively simple finishes on figures up to 1:32 scale. Artist's oils have excellent blending qualities, but are not easy to apply to smaller scale models, and it is not always possible to obtain matte finishes. Because of the different properties of the paints, some modelers prefer to combine two kinds: for example, using oils for a realistic sheen on skin tones, and enamels for clothing and equipment. Good visual reference material is also a valuable aid to realistic figure painting.

One useful tip if you are a complete beginner to figure painting is to start with figures that have plain uniforms – for example a soldier in a single color navy blue dress suit – rather than trying to paint complex multicolored and braided dress uniforms. Another useful tip is to start with some of the cheaper plastic figures, and develop your painting skills on them before spending money on more expensive and intricate metal figures. While most modelers think of figure painting in a military context, as these examples show, any railroad or diorama modeler also needs to be proficient at figure painting. Civil figures need the same painting techniques as the more elaborate military figures.

1 Apply an undercoat of neutral gray to the entire figure and the horse to unify the different components. Then paint a coat of sandy yellow on all of the flesh areas of the human figure and on other light-toned parts, such as the tan-colored leather and the bright fabric, because in these cases the gray would result in subdued shades or require additional layers of paint.

3 Finish the clothes and accoutrements by dry-brushing and blending increasingly lighter shades of the base colors. Lighten bright colors, such as red, with yellow rather than white. The horse's skewbald markings are achieved with an airbrush capable of detail work, loaded with finely pigmented paint, such as liquid acrylic or airbrushing ink. The beadwork and the shield symbols are handpainted in enamels.

2 Add a thin application of dark red-brown to all of the exposed human skin. Paint over this a blend of various yellows, mid-browns, flesh colors, and white – sometimes mixing them while wet – until you achieve a suitable skin tone. Apply the base colors for all of the clothing beginning with darker shades of the final color, and working gradually from dark to light.

1 Apply an undercoat of neutral gray. This unifies the various materials (plastic kit and epoxy putty, for example). It also acts as a witness coat, and provides a good basis for the colors of regular clothing. Next, apply a layer of sandy yellow to areas of exposed skin.

2 Continue treating the skin areas, beginning with a thin application of dark red-brown to emphasize lowlights. When this is dry, add a blend of various yellows, mid-browns, flesh colors, and white until you achieve the desired effect. Apply the base colors for all of the clothes. Use darker shades of the final color so that you do not need to add separate lowlights.

3 The finished effect is achieved by repeated dry-brushing and careful blending of lightened base colors until all of the detail can be seen and there are visible highlights. The final touches, such as buttons and facial hair, are then painted in.

Above A World War II scene. The tank and figures are from standard kits, extensively detailed and remodeled. Paint effects such as the camouflage finish were achieved with an airbrush, with some dry-brushing to obtain highlights.

Left This figure is the engineer of a Victorian open-cabbed locomotive. The work is a substantial rebuild of a 1:32 scale plastic military figure, carefully painted using artist's oil paints.

Vehicles and machinery

The modeling of vehicles and other pieces of machinery is justifiably popular, whether they are for domestic, commercial, or military use. Just as the shape and detailing of automobiles can have a strong appeal in the real world, the same is true of models. Trucks and buses may not generally be as sleekly attractive as sports cars, but they have a chunky charm that the aficionado finds every bit as compelling.

Military vehicles belong to two distinct categories: those used for the transportation of personnel and freight; and AFVs – armored fighting vehicles. Transportation trucks are often military versions of vehicles used in civilian life, but AFVs are obviously specialized, including tanks and other pieces of mobile weaponry.

Model railroaders confront a challenge not usually faced by other transport modelers, because their locomotives are expected to function like the prototype. They must be capable of movement in their own right and have the ability to haul other items of rolling stock. This means that railroaders must consider more than the appearance of their models: wheels must be the correct gauge and stay on the track, axles must run true, and propulsion systems must be effective and controllable.

All models must portray the features that reflect their historical period. Such details are just as important for vehicles and machinery as the correct items of uniform are for a figure. Do not ignore the need for research – far from being a chore, it can be an enjoyable and rewarding part of a modeling project.

Modifying a tank

Above The Sherman M4 tank, complete with modifications and painted.

This project modifies a standard, commercially produced 1:35 scale kit for an M4 Sherman tank. Simple materials, including styrene strip and two-part epoxy putty, are used to adapt the shape and build on additional details. The result is transformation of the tank into a vehicle that looks poised for action – or recently returned from combat.

Checklist

Materials

Plastic kit, Styrene strip, Styrene solvent, Two-part epoxy putty, Toilet tissue, Diluted white glue, X-Acto handle and blade, Miniature sculpting tools, Piece of fine mesh gauze, ½in (12mm) brush for glue

1 Assemble the basic tank kit, except for the tracks.

2 Glue a beam of styrene along the side of the tank with styrene solvent. The length should be an exact fit along the side panel.

3 Add smaller section styrene strip over the beam. This begins the framework which will contain the sandbags. Build on more strips to form a cage on the side of the vehicle.

5 Mix the two-part epoxy putty following the manufacturer's instructions, and roll it into a long thin strip. Cut the strip into pieces the length of scale sandbags.

7 Begin by placing the sandbags on the tank. They should be placed to follow the contours of the tank.

4 Add a beam of styrene at the front of the tank. Build a cage of thin styrene strip on to the front, as you did at the side. The tracks can now be fitted.

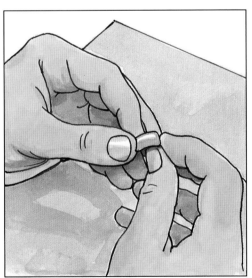

6 Shape the pieces into sandbags.

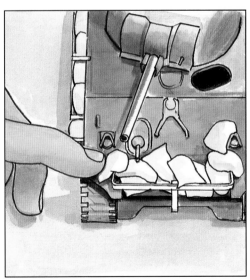

8 Continue this work at the front of the vehicle. While the putty remains soft, you can drape the sandbag and allow it to fall into shape. Push the sacks gently into place.

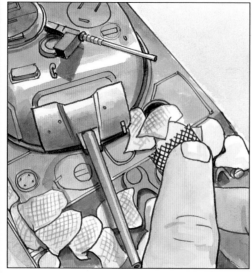

9 Use a small piece of gauze to imprint texture on the surface of the sandbags. The result may be over scale, but conveys the impression of sacking.

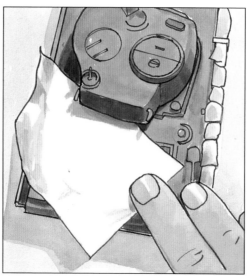

11 Position a piece of toilet tissue to portray a tarpaulin draped over the rear of the vehicle.

13 This molds the paper to the shape of the vehicle.

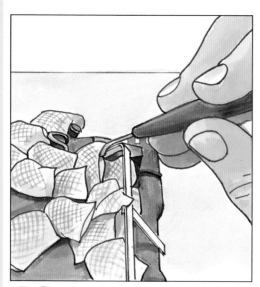

10 Make indentations with a modeling tool to represent the seams of the sandbags.

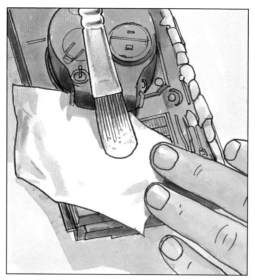

12 Fix the paper in place by soaking it with diluted white glue applied with a brush.

14 Apply a second piece of toilet tissue in the same way, and allow it to dry.

European tramway locomotive

Above The finished tramway locomotive pauses on a 1:34 scale narrow gauge railway layout.

Narrow gauge railroads of between 2ft and 3ft (60–90cm) are popular modeling subjects in Britain and continental Europe. This steam tram engine shows how a pleasing model can be constructed with simple techniques, using sheet styrene and some commercial parts. Although in 1:34 scale, the locomotive looks right, and because it is built around a functioning chassis it is an effective working model.

Checklist

Materials
60 thou (1.5mm) and 40 thou (1mm) thick styrene sheet, Styrene strip in various sizes, Suitable working chassis, Commercial whitemetal fittings, 30 thou (0.75mm) diameter brass rod, Suitably sized bolt for fixing to chassis, Figure for engineer, Styrene solvent/glue, Two-part epoxy glue, Enamel or acrylic paints, Ruler, H or 2H pencil, Cutting mat, Try square, X-Acto handle and blades, Metal straight-edge, Airbrush, Small paintbrushes

1 Choose an electrically powered chassis (ours is a Fleischmann 0–6–0), and sketch the locomotive you want to fit to it. This locomotive was inspired by the type used in Europe and manufactured by such companies as Hohenzollern, Henschell, Kraus, and Maffei. The model will represent a 2ft (60m) gauge loco in 1:34 scale, running on 16.5mm (HO) track.

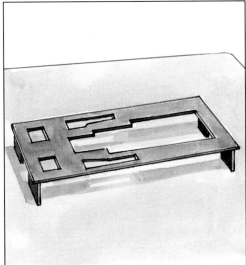

2 Cut a deck from a piece of 60 thou (1.5mm) thick styrene sheet. Make holes in this to clear the motor and parts of the valve gear. Because deck edges can easily be knocked during use and have their paint chipped off, it is better to choose black styrene than white. Add pilot beams at front and rear in the same material.

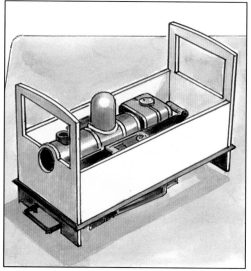

3 Test the deck section on the chassis. A strip of styrene inside the rear pilot beam hooks under a lug on the rear of the chassis, and a bolt goes through the deck into an existing tapped hole in the chassis for final fixing. Test run the chassis on the railroad layout to check clearances and make sure that the motor and valve gear are not obstructed.

5 Glue the tramway body onto the deck, and fit the boiler unit, using a suitable solvent. The existing dome on this boiler was too small, so a commercial whitemetal dome was fitted over it and fixed with epoxy glue. Attach the unit to the chassis again, and test run to check that operation is not impaired.

7 Give the locomotive a basic coat of paint using an airbrush before adding the engineer and fitting the roof. This is made of 30 thou (0.75mm) thick styrene. Curve it by taping it to a jar or can of suitable diameter and putting it in hot water.

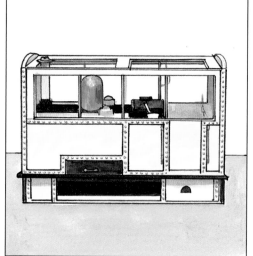

4 Cut the tram casing from a 60 thou (1.5mm) thick styrene sheet, and weld the pieces with a suitable solvent. Make openings in the ends and a hole at the front for the smokebox door. The smokebox, boiler, and firebox for this model were cut from the body part of a commercial tank locomotive obtained secondhand.

6 Build up the rest of the bodywork. The skirts that partly obscure the wheels are made from styrene sheet and strips of styrene embossed with rivets. Handrails and stanchions for the roof are cut from 30 thou (0.75mm) diameter brass rod. The smokestack is a styrene tube, and pieces of styrene and brass rod represent the controls. The whitemetal tank fillers are commercial items.

8 Fit commercial (non-working) lamps onto brackets formed from L-shaped pieces of 30 thou (0.75mm) diameter brass rod at each end of the locomotive.

Above A view during construction of a Mallet-style locomotive in 1:34 scale. The chassis and smokebox/boiler unit are commercial products. The rest of the construction is styrene sheet, with brass wire additions and some modified whitemetal boiler fittings.

Above A passenger car in the process of construction. The interior is fully detailed before the roof is fixed.

Above Using modified commercial chassis, the bodies of these two open cars were built from styrene sheet and strip. The left-hand car was painted a basic gray and black, and on the right we see the appearance after lettering and light weathering.

Detailing an American diesel locomotive

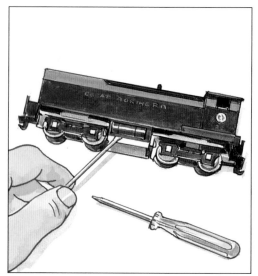

2 Remove the body to facilitate the fitting of the parts supplied and the additional details. Use a screwdriver to lever each side of the belly fuel tank and release the lugs that hold the body in place. It then just lifts off.

Above A less than pristine diesel switcher at work on a layout, moving a grimy boxcar into the local freight yard. This typical sight can be created on any model rail layout, and by adding crew figures, weathering, and extra details to the classic Athearn Baldwin S12 switcher you can considerably increase the realism.

Virtually everything you need for building a model railroad layout in the popular scales is available from model railroad suppliers, but the models you purchase are shiny new and sometimes lack the touches distinctive to particular companies. You can increase the character of your models by adding or improving details, and giving them a worn "in service" look. A typical example is this Athearn Baldwin S12 diesel switcher, an excellent choice for a small HO layout or for a relative newcomer to modeling.

The real locomotive was sold to many American railroads and the model comes in the colors of several of them. This one depicts the five S12s purchased by the Great Northern Railway in 1953 and withdrawn in 1968, the numbers being 24–28. It was used for yard switching, and local freight.

Checklist

Materials
Craft knife, Fine file or emery board, Tweezers, Pin drill, Small staples or grabrail detail parts (from model railroad suppliers), Cyanoacrylate glue, Small screwdrivers, Crew figures, Decals

1 When taken from the box the model looks like this: a body on the powered chassis, and a bag containing handrails, detail fittings, and coupler parts, all to be fixed to the basic model. An "exploded" diagram shows where the parts fit.

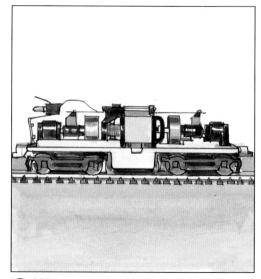

3 Without the body, the chassis and power unit are revealed. The motor is fitted centrally, in line with the body securing lugs. There is a big brass flywheel in each drive train. These, and the gearing to all of the axles, along with the weight of the metal chassis, give this locomotive a superb performance. Clip the couplers and their metal securing plates to the coupler mounts projecting at each end. You can use magnetic couplers if you prefer.

4 The body after removal from the chassis. Just as it is easier to fit the couplers to the separated chassis, so it is easier to detail and complete the body shell when it is independent. The body has a good basic paint scheme but no small lettering. The side grabrails are molded on, and the lightbox (above the "AT" of the company name) is not painted in.

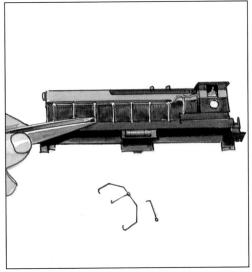

6 Return the cab molding to the body and clip it back in place. Sort out and fit all the handrails, stanchions, and lengths, and attach them to the walkway sides. The stanchions are preformed and thread over the handrails. Tweezers are useful for inserting the stanchions into their tiny locating holes. If any holes are too small, open them a little with the pin drill. The end handrails can be seen partly assembled below the loco body.

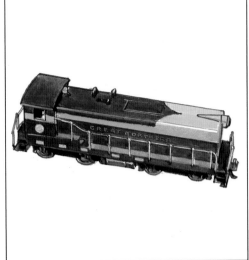

8 Glue the bell and horn that come with the model. This locomotive also needs an orange warning beacon just in front of the cab, and this was made from a plastic dummy light from a road vehicle accessory pack. You could use a piece of orange scrap plastic instead. The grabrails are needed right side only – leave the left side plain. Paint the five yellow warning panels on each walkway valance, or use yellow decal strips, as was done here.

5 Unclip the cab molding, slide out the glazing block from inside, and cut away the side window areas with your craft knife. Glue the two crew figures of your choice inside the cab. Use a craft knife and fine file to remove the molded plastic grabrails (rungs) on either side of the hood. Add wire grabrails from the details pack (or from shortened office staples), using a pin drill to pierce the locating holes. Glue the rungs from the inside.

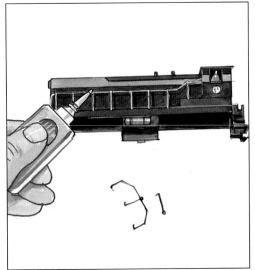

7 A touch of cyanoacrylate glue, used very sparingly, will hold all the stanchions firmly in place. It is a good idea to do this even if they appear to be a snug fit already, because it will save any chance of their working loose later on. The glue dispenser shown is particularly useful for modeling since it can be finely controlled by finger pressure to release tiny drops of glue only, avoiding the risk of "flooding" the model and ruining it.

9 Carry out the finishing touches. Paint all the handrails dark green, picking out the light box on the hood side in black (and adding a small number 25). Attach a red fire warning notice on each side. Put in rain and dirt "runs" over the paintwork. Paint the handrails on each side of the end steps in matte white, and the armrest in each side window light brown.

Steam locomotives

Above Careful detail work and the addition of a dirty weathered finish transforms this model from the shiny plastic original.

2 Some models have poorly defined detail parts. On this tank engine, the original plastic molded safety valves forward of the cab were cut off and replaced with a metal casting. The reversing rod on the boiler side was similarly replaced, and a prominent mold mark on the cab roof was filed down.

Model steam locomotives have finely molded plastic bodies, but new models with metal bodies are still being produced. When purchased, the models are gleaming and impeccable, just like a brand new locomotive fresh from the builder.

Some enthusiasts prefer them this way, and collectors especially like to keep them in a glossy display condition. However, when locomotives work hard they inevitably become weathered and dirty. These effects can be impressively reproduced in miniature. Sometimes models lack sufficient detail, and this can be added, as can crew figures. It is also possible to alter some models slightly to produce slight variants. Typical work and changes are shown here.

Checklist

Materials

Craft knife, Fine file or emery board, Tweezers, Small paintbrush, Pin drill, Universal glue and cyanoacrylate glue and cement, Staples or wire, Plastic rod and plastic strip, Imitation coal, Miniature crew figures, Cast parts if required (e.g. safety valves, whistles, domes, etc.), Cardboard, Paints (especially brown, earth, black and gray)

1 Use a small paintbrush and a mixture of earth, black, and gray paints to add a dirt and grease effect to the wheels and side motion, the chassis sides, brake gear, and cylinders. Apply the paint very lightly and be careful not to allow any on the wheel tread or electrical pickups.

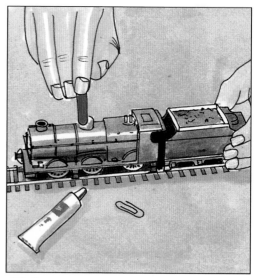

3 Some more typical improvements. On this locomotive, plastic strip was used to depict the added rails which increase the tender capacity. Here, a mold line is being rubbed off the steam dome with an emery board. A paper clip in the foreground will replace the tender drawbar to couple the tender closer to the locomotive.

4 A more extensive alteration is shown here. This German Class 94 tank engine had its original vented cab roof removed and replaced by a rounded cab roof made from a strip of cardboard. Tweezers are used to hold the new parts in place while the glue sets. The coal bunker was also altered with cardboard to depict a sheet metal finish instead of the wood finish on the original.

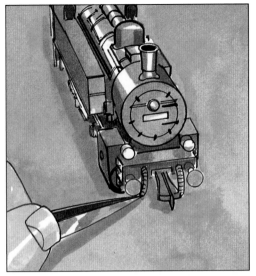

6 Many steam locomotive models omit the flexible steam and brake pipes on the pilot beams or pilots. Model stores sell these as accessories, but you can also cut them from a guitar G-string (sold in music stores), using pliers. You will need tweezers to help you glue them in place. (Note: This applies to models in HO or larger only.)

8 Some models are supplied with engineer and fireman figures for the cab, but they are missing from most models. Crew figures are available in model stores, but sometimes they must be trimmed to fit inside the cab. Ours is an extreme case, because the motor of this small locomotive fills the cab.

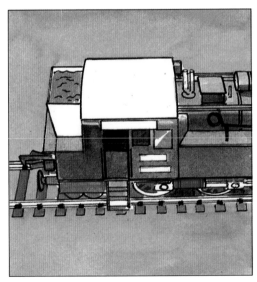

5 The same locomotive now has new number plates made form cardboard on the cab side, and a rolled strip of tissue above the door to depict a canvas side-screen carried on the real loco.

7 Another common omission is certain handrails or grabrails. Or they may be molded as plastic ridges only, which you can pare away carefully with a craft knife. Insert and glue wire rails into pre-drilled holes, as shown on the end of this tank locomotive. Water pipes were also added to the rear of the cab on this model.

9 The same locomotive with the engineer glued inside the cab, and dummy coal glued on top of the plastic coal in the bunker, with a tiny shovel glued on top. Dirt and weathering is painted lightly over the locomotive sides, and water stains run below the filler caps.

Scratchbuilt boat

This boat is an important feature of a model railroad layout. A flat-bottomed waterline model, built to the scale of 1:34, it is selectively compressed but retains the distinctive character of the original. Around 6in (150mm) was removed from the length, mostly from the hold section, whereas the vertical scale remains approximately correct. The details were completed with commercial parts.

Checklist
Materials
Research materials, ¼in (6mm) thick foamboard, 20 thou (0.5mm) and 40 thou (1mm) thick styrene sheet, Styrene strip, Commercial fittings, Old paintbrush handles, Rigging cord, White glue, Styrene solvent, Cyanoacrylate glue, 30 thou brass wire, Acrylic and/or enamel paints, Office staples, Ruler, H or 2H pencil, Cutting mat, Try square, X-Acto handle and blades, Metal straight-edge, Dressmaking pins, Small brush for solvent, ¼in (6mm) brush, Damp cloth

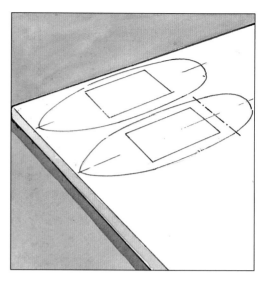

Above The completed boat moored at the quayside.

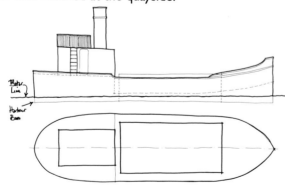

1 Make a full-size outline sketch of the proposed model, comprising a square-on side elevation and a plan view. Only the general outline is needed, because the details will be based on photographs of the real boats. The model is not accurate, because it is under scale in length, but aims to capture the spirit of the original. It will be a static model, berthed at the wharf of a railroad layout for loading from mineral cars.

2 This is a waterline boat – that is, it does not extend much below the waterline – and the hull above this line has vertical sides. Therefore two identical pieces are cut in ¼in (6mm) thick foamboard. Cut a central rectangle from both of them where the hold will be, and cut one piece across the line where the deck level changes.

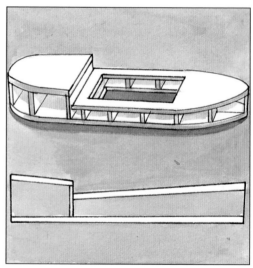

3 Space the deck sections above the boat part, using additional pieces of ¼in (6mm) thick foamboard. In this case, the two deck sections slope toward the middle of the boat.

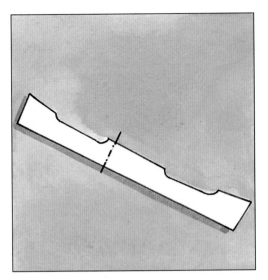

4 Using the plan view as a guide, calculate the total perimeter of the boat, and cut an equal length of 20 thou (0.5mm) thick styrene sheet. For this large-scale model a single length was not available, and a join was made on the non-viewing side (the back) of the boat. After cutting, shape the top edge of the styrene strip to the profile of the side elevation, remembering to adjust for the fact that the drawing shows it square on.

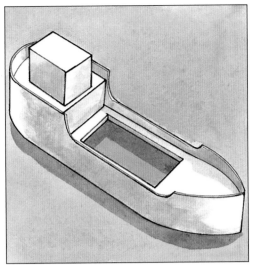

6 Build the deckhouse as a box, made from 40 thou (1mm) thick styrene. Because the deck slopes, it is not square.

8 Begin fitting the details. Here, strips of styrene edge the hull and the hold, and provide piping. A winch in the bows was built mainly from styrene, but includes some whitemetal parts and a wheel from a military vehicle kit.

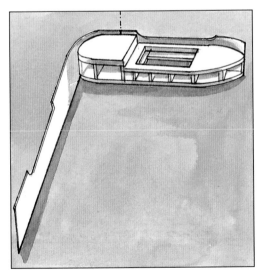

5 Use cyanoacrylate glue to attach the styrene strip around the side of the boat section previously built, making the main join at the bows.

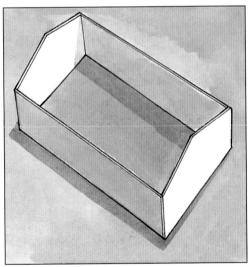

7 Construct an open-topped box with pent ends from 40 thou (1mm) thick styrene sheet. Check that it fits exactly into the hold opening.

9 Details on the deckhouse at the stern include a ladder made from office staples and brass wire. The porthole, ventilators, and the stanchions for the railings are commercial fittings, and the funnel is a tube rolled up from several layers of 10 thou (0.25mm) thick styrene sheet with the join at the back. The bridge was built up in small-section lime stripwood. After painting the rest of the boat, plank the deck in suitable section lime stripwood.

Trucks

Above A US Peterbilt truck – a highly detailed kit, with bunk bed for the driver, and even including the gearshift. There are lots of chrome features, as there are on the real vehicle. Note the airconditioning unit and marker lights on the roof.

Although European vehicles are available, truck kits are dominated by the models of big American trucks. Some molds are over 20 years old but still excellent; they often follow the design of the real thing more closely than modern kits. The fit of the older kits can be a little slack, however, so we deal with the problems which can ruin a good model, such as parts that do not hold firm at the attachment point.

Checklist

Materials
Razor saw, Round file, Craft knife, Sanding block, Knife, Tweezers, Brushes, Steel ruler, Liquid polystyrene glue, Cyanoacrylate glue, Styrene sheet, Card, Paints, Screwdriver, Epoxy glue, Black telephone wire, Spray paints, Masking tape, Two-sided tape, Chrome scotch tape, Rubber bands

■ The engine is normally constructed first. Build the major components, but leave items such as starter motors, alternators, and any pulleys with fan belts. These will be painted different colors, as will exhaust manifolds. The gearbox will probably be mounted onto the engine so it can be painted at the same time. Mount your parts on toothpicks or clothespins; an old paintbrush handle pushed into the propshaft mounting hole is ideal.

2 Spray paints are invaluable for these large assemblies, allowing you to paint individual sections without masking. Automobile paints are available in sprays from hardware and auto stores, but make sure that the paint is not cellulose-based, because this will melt the plastic. The finish on these paints is very glossy, and you can polish them if you wish. Matte colors are also available.

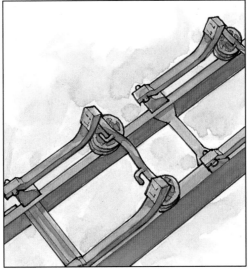

4 While the engine is drying, tackle the chassis. The biggest problem here is to keep it level, so sand the ends of all the cross members flat, and cement these to one side frame. Check at eye level that they are all at 90° to the frame. Place the other frame in position but do not cement it. Tape a flat steel ruler along the inner edge of the frame on top of the cross members.

6 On older kits, location points may be inaccurate, especially on axles. If so, sand off the location pins, attach the parts level, then lightly scrape the joint clean with the back of a knife blade. Fuel tanks can be treated this way also, and if the ends are a separate item, sand the end surface evenly. The end cap will then fit perfectly.

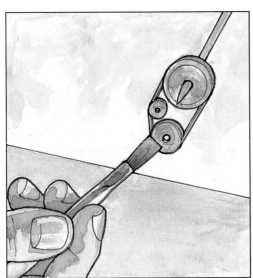

3 Spray your engine in the appropriate color (if you write to the truck manufacturers, they will supply you with a brochure giving the correct color for each part). Paint the smaller details by hand. Use black for the belts, and steel for the exhaust manifold and exhaust side of the turbocharger. Add a little flesh color, dry brushed on, to give a used look.

5 Hold the entire unit together with rubber bands, and rest it on a flat surface. Check for wobble, rectify if needed, and leave to harden overnight with a weight on top. Cement the other frame, and again check for alignment. Put in the suspension and the fuel tank brackets but not the tanks themselves, because it may be difficult to spray behind them.

7 Add all three axles at the same time, and check by eye that they are all in line. Always use a solid piece of board as a base for checking alignment. Make any alterations needed while the glue is still soft. This is vital if your truck is to stand level. When you are satisfied, add any cab mounts, etc.

8 When all the parts have been prepared for painting, spread some old newspaper over your board and make sure that there is plenty of ventilation. Wear a mask if possible. Shake the can well, and spray very light bursts into all the nooks and crannies. Then spray continuously to give overall coverage, building up in a series of light coats.

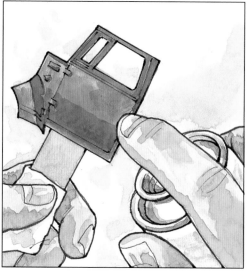

10 If the cab comes in separate parts, you will find it easier to spray each part mounted on a stick with two-sided tape. This means that you will have to take a little extra care when assembling the parts later. Scrape off the paint from the edges and let a brushful of liquid cement trickle in until it is fixed. This eliminates the problems of overspray.

12 The straps for square tanks are mainly flat. Make them from 15 thou styrene sheet cut just short of the full length. Glue a piece of rod at both ends to represent the bolts. All straps have a rubber underlay to prevent the strap from chafing the tank. Construct these from 10 thou styrene sheet just wider than the strap, and paint them black. Drill a hole at each end of the bracket and mount the tank and strap as in step 10.

9 Cabs come in either one piece or several sections. Mount a one-piece cab on a clothes hanger handle and spray one side at a time. Begin across the back in order to practice. Use quick passes approximately 10in (25cm) from the surface. Build up very thin layers to make a strong color rather than applying a thick coat that could suddenly run. Paint sprayed in a warm room will dry quickly.

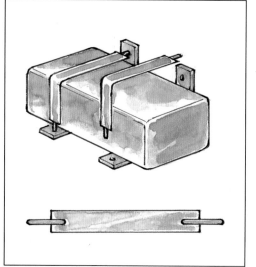

11 Fuel tanks with molded straps rarely look real, so unless they are chrome, sand off the straps and make new ones from rod or strip plastic. Tanks are held onto the brackets by straps looped around either end, trapping the tank beneath. For round straps, drill a hole at the top and bottom of the bracket. Position the tank and pass the rod over it and through each hole. Heat the ends with a hot screwdriver to form a rivet to hold it in place.

13 Wheels come in various styles and sizes, but they all have holes in them to allow air to circulate around the brakes and to make them lighter. Some of these holes may be filled with chrome plating or flash, so open them up with a round file. Twist counter-clockwise to stop it biting too hard. Note where the plastic dust comes to on the file, and ream each hole to the same depth. The front and rear hubs are the same color as the chassis, so handpaint these carefully.

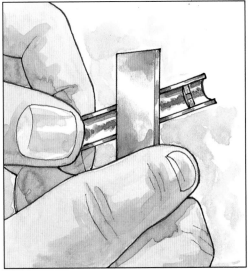

14 Use fine black telephone wire for flexipipes from brake cylinders. Drill two holes in each cylinder, and fix one end of the wire in with epoxy or Cyanoacrylate glue. Then run each in a loop up to the side of the chassis, and glue the other end. For diesel pipes, use bare wire from the tank into the chassis through two tiny holes.

16 Truck kits usually have lots of "chrome" parts in them, and many are halves of major components, such as fuel tanks and exhaust stacks. Although these look shiny, they are often spoiled by bad joints with seams showing. The chrome prevents cement acting on the plastic, so you must remove the chrome from any surfaces to be joined, using a fine sanding block. Be careful not to fracture the outer surfaces. The mating surfaces must be as near a perfect fit as possible.

18 Add the final touches. Due to molding limitations, some parts such as mirror arms and mud flaps, are slightly overscale. Make new arms from flower arranging wire, bent and cut to the size of the original parts. Mud flaps can be cut from 15 thou styrene sheet. Improve mirror faces by adhering a strip of chrome scotch tape on the face and trimming to size. Burnish the tape with a wooden toothpick first. Paint colored lights with clear colored acrylics.

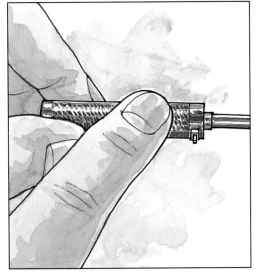

15 On tractor units, there is an air hose connection to the trailer, and these come in two distinct styles. The US types are simple black pipes with couplings on the ends, and some US kits supply black vinyl tubes for this purpose. Europe uses coiled plastic pipes, colored for recognition. Telephone wires in red, blue, and yellow, wrapped around a pencil, make excellent representations. Mount them on a small frame.

17 Hold the halves together and add the liquid cement. Wait a few seconds before pressing them together tightly. The molten plastic should ooze out slightly. Do not touch it yet; wait until it is nearly hard, then roll it off with a finger until it is completely removed. Do not rub too hard or you may remove the chrome. There should now be a good joint, which will only need a touch of silver paint where it was cut from the sprue.

Aircraft

Above The P-51 Mustang was a popular World War II airplane. This model is built from a kit and no special tools are needed.

Aircraft are among the most popular models available in kit form. They give you almost endless creative opportunities, because there are so many real-life models to copy or modify, and so many markings applied by different air forces and units. Exposed to the elements and the stress of high speeds, the finish of airplanes deteriorates daily, so that you can depict models from "new" to "battle-damaged," stopping time at any point you wish. A kit is a jumping-off point for whatever design combinations your imagination suggests.

It is important, however, to undertake some planning before you begin building even the most straightforward kit. Read the instruction sheets fully before you start work, so that you become familiar with the steps involved and tools needed, and you know exactly where you are aiming. This will ensure that you do not get halfway through and find that you have passed the point where you can fit some internal part. It

also gives you the chance to spot any areas where you want to make adaptations.

Planning must include the painting sequence: the parts to paint on sprues (holding frames) before assembly, the interiors, the order in which to paint the camouflage, the colors to use, and which areas to mask if you are using a brush or spray. It is easiest to group together all the parts that need to be painted in one color. Canopies need special treatment: you can achieve sharp, straight lines with the aid of masking tape or masking liquid, or use decal stripes. Decals will be included in the kit, along with insignia, code letters, and other details, but you can individualize your model by choosing alternative decals. There are specialized decal sheets that enable you to change the character of your model completely, and these sometimes include instructions on altering a model to a different marque. The P-51 Mustang was a popular World War II airplane. This model

is built from a kit and no special tools are needed. The joints in plastic kits can sometimes be imperfect. We show you how to overcome this problem, and how to make neat wing and tail angles. Airplane kits may use the terms "dihedral" and "anhedral" for these – referring to the angle between the wing and the horizontal. Most aircraft have a dihedral on the wing, like the P–51, but some have an anhedral on the tail, such as the Harrier and Phantom. The angle is normally built into the model but must be prevented from drooping.

Checklist

Materials
Paints listed in kit, Liquid polystyrene glue, Epoxy putty, Modeling clay, Masking tape, Scotch tape, Blu-Tack, 2ft × 3ft (60cm × 90cm) approx., Modeling board (or hardboard), ¼in (6mm) and ⅛in (3mm) flat brushes, Fine 00 round brush, Old paintbrush for glue, Small drill, Narrow clipper, Craft knife, Grade 3 and 9 sandpaper, Sanding block, Nail files, Toothpicks, Clothespins, Shaving or similar brush, Cocktail stirrer (optional)

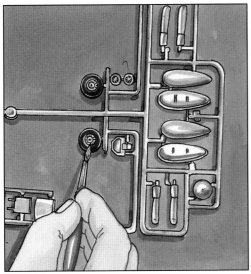

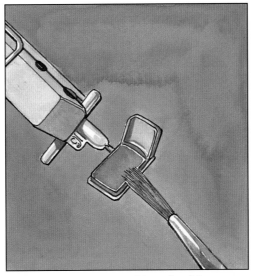

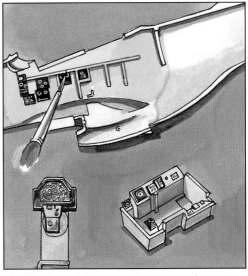

1 Painting is important for the final effect of your model, and care with small components is just as important as the overall camouflage. But these parts might be awkward to hold, so paint them on the sprue frame with the fine brush.

3 Hold the separated length of frame with a clothespin while you apply the paint. After drying, cut off the components with the flat side of the cutters toward them, and touch in any small blemishes.

5 Before gluing any pieces together, check to see what parts of the interior need to be painted. Paint all of the cockpit parts with the correct color as a base coat. Paint the instrument panels and side consoles black. When dry, dry-brush the details, highlighting the raised areas. Dry-brush as follows: dip a flat brush into the paint, then remove most of the paint by wiping on a paper towel. Rub the brush back and forth over the surface and the details will gradually show up.

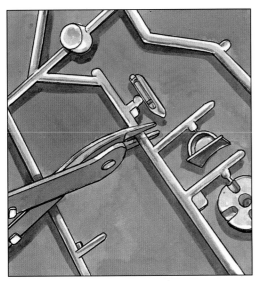

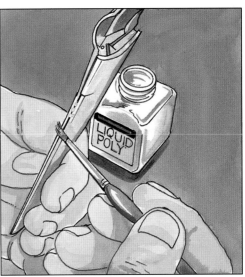

2 Remove from the frame inaccessible elements and those that need complicated painting, retaining the part number. Use sharp clippers, and a thin blade for the smallest items, so that you do not distort them when cutting through the gates.

4 When painting larger parts, it is important to be able to manipulate them without leaving fingermarks. Place a toothpick through the center of a wheel, and spin the wheel against your stationary brush to achieve a neat circle at the edge of the tire. Stand parts on toothpicks in a block of modeling clay to dry. For seats and other components, fix a blob of Blu-Tack on a clothespin and rest the part on it. You can then paint all around it with ease.

6 Apply liquid polystyrene glue with an old small paintbrush. Hold the parts together with the joint vertical, touch the brush in one spot, and allow the liquid to flow along the gap. Repeat until the entire edge is fixed. If glue spills onto the outside surface, blow on it until it disappears but do not touch it until dry or you will leave a smear and spoil the finish.

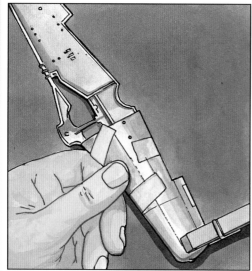

7 Before adding the top halves of a wing, you must decide what load, if any, your plane will carry, because the location holes for pylons and bombs must be opened using a small drill from inside the bottom of the wing. Cement the top half in position with polystyrene glue, then squeeze the joint and clamp in place with tape or a clothespin. Leave to harden overnight.

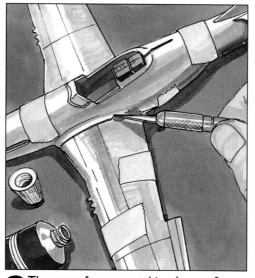

9 The parts from some kits do not fit perfectly and can leave gaps. Overcome this by filling them with body putty from a hobby store. Use a knife blade to push small amounts in the crack. A wing joint is shown here, but the same method can be used to improve any part of your model.

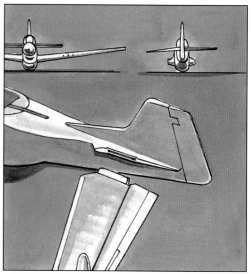

11 The angle of an airplane's tail and wings may be dihedral (normally upward) or anhedral (normally downward). The P–51 has a dihedral angle, which is built into the model. When the wings are glued and left to dry, however, they can easily droop.

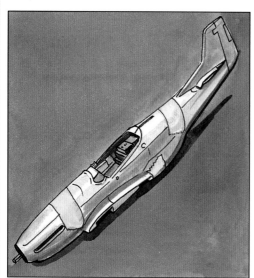

8 Several units normally need to be trapped between the halves of the fuselage. The advantage of using liquid glue is that you can position these before gluing and relocate any part that becomes dislodged. Again, hold the joint vertical, add the glue, squeeze the parts, and clamp with tape. Never apply the tape first, because the cement can seep under it and mar the surface.

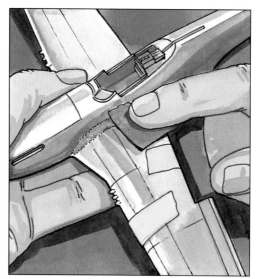

10 When the putty is hard, smooth off the excess with progressively finer sandpaper until the joint is filled level with either side. If the panel lines on the kit are raised, take care not to destroy these. Test the results by painting some matte gray over the area, which will reveal any blemishes that still need attention.

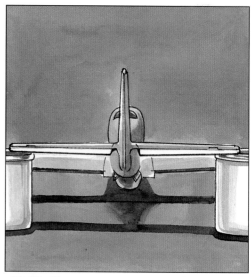

12 One way to overcome the problem is to place a blob of Blu-Tack on the bottom of the fuselage and place it on a flat surface. Make sure that the fin is vertical, and when both tails or wings are cemented, place two paint cans or wooden blocks underneath and adjust until both sides are level. Leave overnight. Any convenient pair of supports can be used provided they are identical so that the tips of the tails are equal in height.

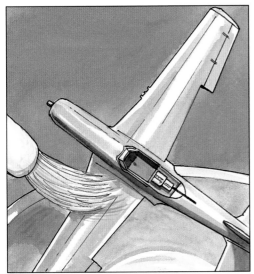

13 Paint will not adhere satisfactorily to a surface that is dusty or marked with grease from your fingers where you held a part during assembly. As a precaution, wash your model in warm water mixed with a drop of dishwashing detergent using a shaving or similar brush. Rinse under a cold faucet and leave to dry in the air. Do not attempt to dry with a towel or paper, because this will leave a residue of fluff.

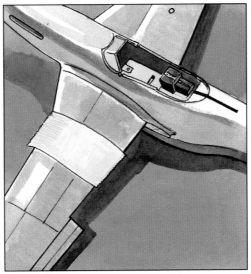

15 Repeat for each window, but do not add the clear parts to the model yet. Never use Scotch tape to mask painted areas such as the stripe on the wing. The easiest way to do this is to paint the white area roughly in place first. Then cut a strip of low-tack tape, such as masking or drafting tape, to the right width, and mask the area of white in its correct position.

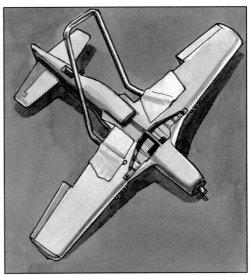

17 Prepare to paint your model by gathering together all the parts that need to be painted in one color. Mount them on toothpicks or clothespins and place in the box lid. This will ensure that you do not miss any pieces. Check that you can hold the main model without your fingers touching the wet paint. You can adapt holding devices from old paintbrush handles and wire coat hangers.

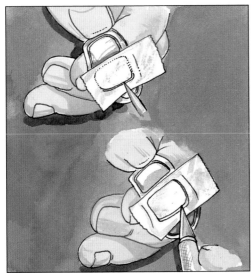

14 Items such as canopies and windshields need masking before you can paint or spray. Cut small strips of Scotch tape and cover one window at a time. Use a toothpick to tuck the tape completely into the edges of the frames. Trim around the frames with a modeling knife and remove the excess carefully.

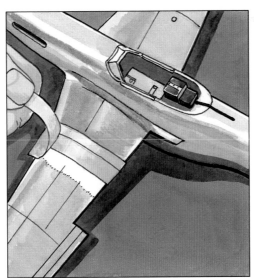

16 Paint the main color with the tape in place. If using a brush, begin a little way from the edge of the masking tape and work toward it. This will prevent a buildup of paint forming a ridge. When the paint is dry, carefully peel away the tape by folding it back over itself to reduce the risk of removing any paint. The masking method is much simpler than trying to paint the lines after the main color is on, and is equally useful for creating cheat lines on airliners and around locomotive boilers.

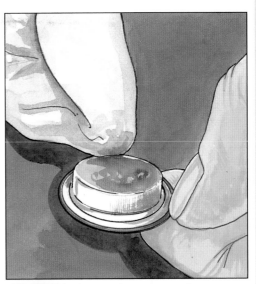

18 Painting can be messy unless you take precautions. First, wipe the can lid clean with some paper towel. This stops a buildup around the can neck that allows the paint to harden. Stir the paint thoroughly – use a cocktail stirrer if possible. When using a brush to apply paint, prime, but do not overload the bristles. Spread the paint evenly and do not brush over an area twice, because you will lift the "skin" of the paint and ruin the finish.

Basic rules of painting

Above F–4E Phantom Israeli camouflage is a good scheme to show, because the colors are distinctive. The model was airbrushed freehand, using the lightest color first. Areas such as the nose cone, cockpit canopy, and tail section needed masking.

This is a pastime to be enjoyed, so the first rule is never to rush. Have a little patience: your model will look infinitely better and more time will have flown than you thought possible.

Gather some reference material before you begin. Magazines are a good source of photographs and drawings, but libraries can supply the big expensive reference books that provide much more information. You cannot help but increase your interest in the subject, and again a better model will result.

Always work in a clean area and keep your hands clean. One of your biggest problems will be getting rid of fingerprints. Read the instruction sheets before you begin, and you will avoid many potential mistakes.

Stir the paint before using and do not assume that your can of paint is at the correct consistency. Brush some on a spare piece of plastic: the paint should become even and the brushmarks disappear in a few seconds. If it does not, add a few drops of the appropriate thinner until the paint covers well and uniformly. Never mix old thinners with the paint – be sure to use the one recommended by the manufacturer. Do not paint cellulose over enamel, because the solvent will destroy the paint below and eat into the plastic.

When painting for some time stir the paint occasionally so that it does not settle.

Wash the brush in thinner every now and then to prevent the hair from clogging with hardened paint. Make sure that all the paint is removed from the ferrule end, and as soon as you finish painting, wash the brush thoroughly, and put it away in a clean box. Do not wait until later!

Checklist

Materials
Low tack masking tape, Scotch tape, Blu-Tack, Masking liquid, Wire cutters, Pliers, Two sizes of flat paintbrush, 1 "00" round paintbrush, HB pencil, Paints as listed in the kit, Wire coathanger

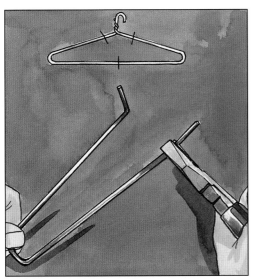

1 Before painting, make sure that the board is clear and clean. Cover it with kitchen paper. Check that the model is dust-free, and that you have a hand hold. If you cannot hold it, construct a handle from an old wire coat hanger. Use wire cutters to cut as shown, and bend the last inch (25mm) at 90° with pliers.

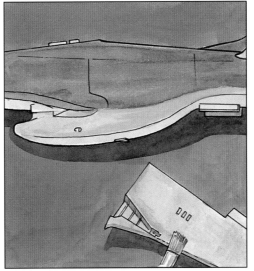

3 Begin by painting the upper surface. Use a large flat brush, and divide the work into sections. Paint a complete part at a time, e.g. a wing, or fuselage, or tail planes. Make sure that there are no bare patches, and overlap the area where the lower color meets the upper to ensure there are no gaps between the two. Be especially careful with wings, where the top color can sometimes wrap around under the leading edge.

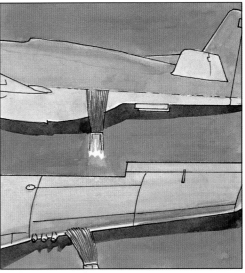

5 Some aircraft have tricky nooks and crannies on the underside. Always try to paint these first. Once you have established the color in these areas, you can brush an even coat over the rest of the surface much more easily. Demarcation lines between colors are best tackled by moving the flat side of the brush sideways along the lines. The edges of wings and tail planes are easy if you hold the brush vertical and move it along the edge.

2 You will now be able to spread the "feet" to any width required and tape them to an unpainted area of the model, so that it is evenly balanced and easy to handle. Familiarize yourself with the color scheme provided on the instruction sheet.

4 Once you are satisfied with the painting, check that you have done all of the tiny bits that require the same color. To avoid trapping dust in the wet paint, place the model in the tray of the kit box and rest the lid on top at a slight angle. This will also enable air to flow freely and dry the paint. Leave overnight, then remove your holder and paint the lower color. While holding the top painted surface, place a soft tissue between it and your fingers.

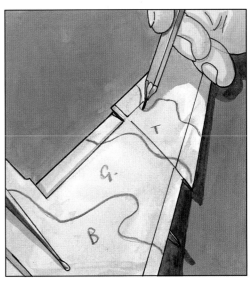

6 The instruction sheet will give the precise pattern for your model. Hold your model over the color plan and draw the lines between the colors with a soft lead pencil. If the pattern is complicated, mark the initial letter of the color in each area. Brush off any pencil dust and fill in the areas. Always start the loaded brush approximately $\frac{1}{8}$in (3mm) from a line and brush out toward it to prevent a buildup where the colors meet.

Decals

Above It is important to make sure that long decals are straight, and to take care not to stretch them. In a few areas where there were compound curves, paint was matched to the decals.

Manufacturers provide decals as the easiest form of decoration for any model – truck, car, tank, or airplane. They recognize that few modelers can paint such complicated designs by hand. Manufacturers go to great lengths to research their subjects and ensure that the model is a faithful replica. As plastic kit modeling has progressed, specialist decal companies have produced alternative decal markings from those in the box. These can be fairly colorful and sometimes carry markings for several machines. You can also buy sheets of solid color decal, strips of different widths, and checkered decal – all in a variety of popular colors.

Most decals slide on with water, but there are also rub-down decals. The first type need to be soaked in a bowl of tepid water for approximately 45 seconds – any longer and the glue will dilute, so that the decal will not adhere to your model. Never leave them just floating around. The rub-downs only need to be accurately placed before you rub over them and release them from the backing sheet.

Prepare the surface before applying either type of decal. As you become more experienced, you may want to use gloss model paints that exactly match the colors used by particular armed forces. Until then, coat your matte paint with acrylic varnish. This provides the smooth finish to which decals adhere best. It also helps to eliminate "silvering": air trapped under the clear decal film.

Checklist

Materials
Sheet of decals, Scissors, Knife blade, Tweezers, Bowl, Soft brush, Soft cloth

Many manufacturers provide only basic schemes, but specialist sheets are available from your local hobby store.

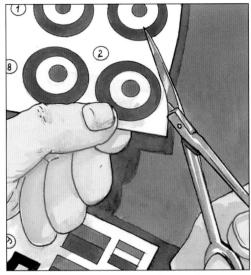

2 Most decal sheets have a number or letter beside each design. These correspond to the same marks on the decal plan. You must make a note of these, because a lot of insignia look very similar but there may be subtle differences – in size, for example. As you place each decal on the model, check its number off on the decal plan with a red pen. It will then be easier to spot any that you may have missed.

4 For letters with film in the center, such as A or O, run a knife blade around the inner edge of the letter, without cutting through the paper backing. Then when the decal is wet, the film will lift off before you place the letter in position. Never attempt to cut a decal that is already wet. When you are ready to apply your decal, half-fill a bowl with tepid water.

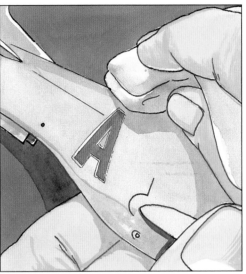

6 If the decal needs repositioning, use the soft wet brush to move it. Dab off any excess water with a damp cloth, and press the decal down firmly with a pad of cloth. This should press the decal into any panel lines or rivets. For that painted-on look, leave the model to dry thoroughly.

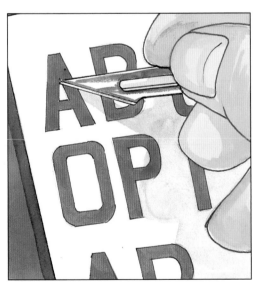

3 Cut out only one or two decals at a time. If you have left- and right-handed designs, affix one before you cut out the next. Trim the design as closely as possible, removing any decal film that extends more than 1/32in (1mm).

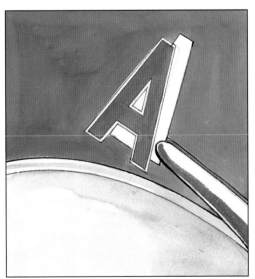

5 Dip your decal for a few moments. Then rest it on the side to soak thoroughly. When it is ready, you should be able to slide it around on the backing paper. Move it to one side just enough to hold the backing paper with tweezers. Shake off any excess water, and place the decal in position. Hold it steady with a soft brush and slide the paper out carefully in any direction that will not crease the design.

7 If by next morning the decals have lifted from the lines or rivets, you may need to use one of the decal solutions available from hobby stores. Spread the solution over the decal with a soft brush and leave it untouched overnight. At first the decal will shrivel up slightly and look a mess. Do not worry – tomorrow it will be tight and flat. Dampen the area around the decal to remove any trace of glue or solvent, and dry with soft cloth.

Vacuforms

Above This Westland Wyvern was made from a vacuform kit, and contains resin and white-metal parts for detailed internal panels (consoles) and seats. The aircraft is in Suez campaign markings.

The vacuform kit is commonly seen as a challenge, and some modelers stay away from them. But once you have built a vacuform, you will treat them like any other kit. Vacuforms provide models that the larger manufacturers think will not arouse sufficient interest to justify the thousands of dollars it costs to cut a steel mold for an injection-molded kit. The vacuforms are generally made on a small scale with master casts of wood or epoxy resin, which will withstand a fair amount of wear and tear. Sheets of plastic are heated and sucked down onto or into the molds to give a true reproduction of the master.

To make the kit, you must first cut the shapes accurately from the sheet of plastic. When that is done you are at a similar stage to starting an injection kit, because nowadays nearly all vacuform interiors come as

molded pieces in white metal or resin. They simply fit inside with only a light rub to clean up the moldings.

Good instructions are the norm these days, and decal sheets are very comprehensive, but do not attempt a complex kit until you have built a few basic models.

A vacuform will test your skills and patience, but with a little care, and by reading the instruction sheet fully, you will be able to sail through it.

Checklist

Materials
Plasticard, Craft knife and sharp blade, Fineliner pen, Tweezers, Files: round, half round, flat and square, Sanding block and rough and fine sandpaper, Liquid cement

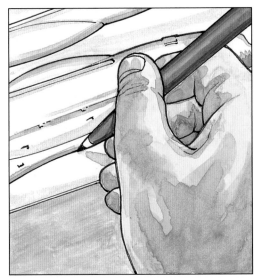

2 The first task is to identify all of the parts. Then the main sheets need to be cut out. Use a pen to draw around the outline of the raised parts, keeping the pen tight in the corners of the molding.

4 Apertures for the cockpit, nose or exhaust pipes are plugged with a crosshatched bulge. Do not cut this away until you have sanded the edges. Use a rough paper to sand the inside edges until the ink outline shows through. Then rub with fine sandpaper until the thin "collar" falls away. You are now at the correct size and shape for the parts to fit together perfectly.

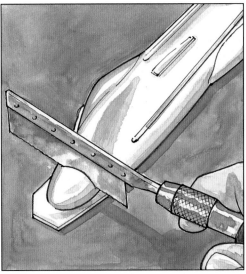

6 Remove the fuselage plugs with a razor saw or knife until the opening is clear, with no rough edges. Because the plastic is thin and does not offer much of an area to cement together, reinforce joints by adding small strips of 20 thou plasticard at intervals along the seam. Bend them to keep the shape of the curve you are joining.

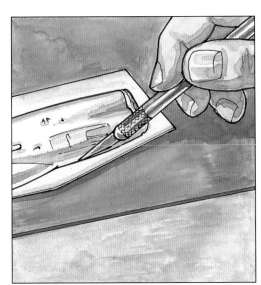

3 Using a sharp blade, score around the part leaving a generous margin outside the ink outline, and crack it free from the main sheet. Then score carefully along the ink outline at a 45° angle, and snap the part out of the sheet. Sand the excess plastic until the part is back to the line shown above.

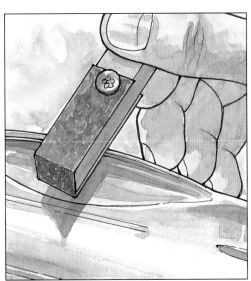

5 Keep checking the fit of the parts, and only sand a little at a time until they fit well. Wings need a little extra sanding on trailing edges to make the two halves very thin, just like the real thing. Take care not to break through the surface, and do not use too much glue or you will melt the plastic.

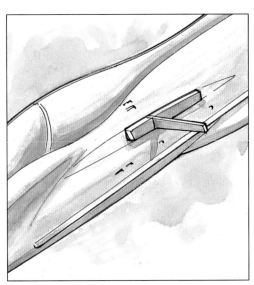

7 Once all the interiors are in position you can start to glue the fuselage. Use liquid glue sparingly and tape the joints. Be careful not to exert too much pressure or you may distort the shape. Some kits give "formers" to maintain the correct shape, but these can easily move when you are assembling the parts. You may also need to add spars to support the wings. From this point on, assembly is as straightforward as in a regular molded kit.

Gallery

As this book demonstrates there are virtually no limits to the modelmaking hobby. You can work from scratch, assemble kits made from various materials, or even collect models made or manufactured by others. The best results are achieved by a combination of careful workmanship and imaginative finishing and display.

Looking at the work of other modelers is extremely useful as it will help you develop your own ideas about materials, techniques, and subjects for modeling. In the Gallery section we give you the opportunity to do this, presenting examples of fine work by some of today's leading modelers to show the high standards that can be achieved.

Examples shown in this section are designed to give you an indication of the diversity of modelmaking. You will notice that working within a particular theme, such as military or aircraft modeling, does not limit you to a particular technique or material.

Materials, methods, and components used in one area of modelmaking can often be transferred to another with very positive results. This approach will enable modelers who specialize in locomotives or figures for example, to gain ideas for placing models in a background context.

It is worth noting that many of the models here are made from readily available kits sold by model stores. The skill of the builder is what makes them distinctive, and this is particularly true of diorama work where truly artistic imagination achieves the best results.

Left and above Impressive modeling created this town on the Milltown and Mineral Mesa Railroad, set in the 1950s at the time of transition from steam to diesel traction. Arranging the structures on a hillside conveys a busy, crowded impression that makes the town look much bigger than it really is. (Model by Bob Lunde)

Left A realistic street scene in Rico, Colorado, on the On3 Rio Grande Southern shows buildings made of cast plaster, wood and styrene. Natural soils were used for the terrain. (Model by Duane Danielson).

Below A British street scene of the 1930s in 1:76 scale. The shop windows are fully detailed and there is an interesting display of the metal advertisements that were once a characteristic of British towns.

Above A realistic city atmosphere created in 1:87 (HO) scale. Modeling of a high order was used here, with some scratchbuilding and some kit building or adaptation. Fire plugs, telephone poles, lampposts, and faded billboards and store signs create a superb "downtown" look. (Model by Bob Lunde)

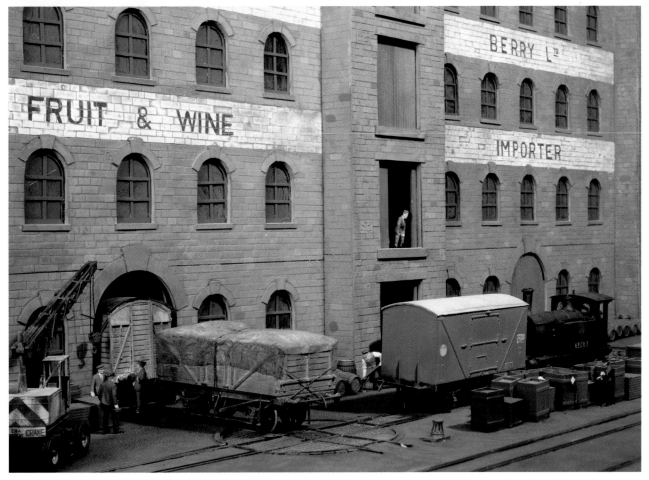

Left A rarely modeled center of interest is the turntable and capstan for positioning railroad cars inside the warehouse for loading. This was once a system much used in Europe, and a few examples remained in the 1950s – the period modeled here. The warehouse dates from the 19th century. (Model by Brian and Philip Parker)

Above The green, rolling hills of the Appalachian highlands are nicely represented in these views of the HO scale modeling being done by the members of the Pittsburgh Model Railroad Museum in Pittsburgh, Pennsylvania. This is an accurate representation of Helmstetter's Curve – a famous location on the Western Maryland Railroad.

Above This little diorama illustrates the kind of fairly simple landscape that can be incorporated into any model layout. A rocky cutting is set in front of a mountain backscene, and in the foreground some men repair the bridge over a stream. It was built by the Swiss MZZ firm to demonstrate their model trees, backgrounds, and scenic materials.

Left An impressive piece of structure modeling depicting a typical British Victorian village school, complete with walled playground. Only the full-size trees behind it reveal that it is part of an entire street of stone-built structures on a British O gauge layout. (Model by Allan Downes)

Above Seen in the distance, this cottage, nestling in a fold of the land, looks just like the real thing. It is part of the delightful Vale of the White Horse display at the Pendon Museum, England, which recreates an area of the county of Berkshire and also incorporates a Great Western Railway model layout. The scale is 1:76, 4mm (¹⁄₆₄in) to 1ft.

Above Seen in the distance, this cottage, nestling in a fold of the land, looks just like the real thing. It is part of the delightful Vale of the White Horse display at the Pendon Museum, England, which recreates an area of the county of Berkshire and also incorporates a Great Western Railway model layout. The scale is 1:76, 4mm (¹⁄₆₄in) to 1ft.

Above A complete farmyard shows some of the characteristics of rural life in England in the 1920s and 1930s. Of particular interest is the rethatching of the barn in the foreground, necessitating a canvas tarpaulin over the roof while work is in progress. (Model by the Pendon Museum)

Left A delightful farming scene, made to the British scale of 4mm (¹⁄₆₄in) to 1ft, depicts the English countryside in the county of Essex as it was in the 1920s and 1930s. Shredded sisal string was used to depict the wheat, and an old-style tractor-hauled reaper and binder harvests the crops. (Model by Bob Tivendale)

Above A small house modified from a kit, with wood siding and corrugated aluminum roof. The wood was stained and brushed with powdered artist's pastel chalks, then treated with an isopropyl alcohol wash. The broken windows were done with a scriber. The model is O scale (1:48, quarter inch equals one foot), built by Bill Schaumburg.

Left England's Pendon Museum has an outstanding display of meticulous countryside modeling, recapturing the appearance of the Vale of the White Horse area of Berkshire as it looked in the 1920s and 1930s. This model of a thatched cottage and country lane, complete with old-time signpost, is to 1:76 scale.

Right Modeling in O gauge allows for spectacularly realistic detailing because the scale is large. This building with random stone finish, and the conservatory alongside, is a complete scratchbuilt project of distinction. (Model by Allan Downs)

Left This beautifully detailed ¼in (6mm) scale model of a Sears home was built from styrene. In the early part of this century, Sears Roebuck, the large catalog store, sold everything from socks to farm supplies to complete home kits. This O scale model of one of their designs is pictured outdoors on a small diorama. (Model by Julian Cavalier)

Left This model of an industrial building is brought alive by the excellent detailing. Notice the individual rows of roof slates made from paper, the water spouts formed from styrene rod, and the careful work on doors, windows, and the staircase. The scale is 1:76. (Model by David Scott)

Right Reducing structures to the minimum needed to suggest the original is a good space-saving technique. In the larger scales (in this case 1:34), the smallest building still has a lot of impact. This is the depot from the Portpyn layout. Its real size would be about 9ft x 12ft (3m x 4m). Notice the effective use of billboards. (Model by Christopher Payne)

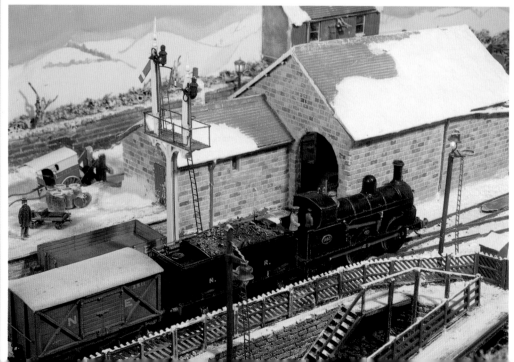

Left Rarely modeled though attractive is a winter setting. This is a country station early in the 20th century. The scratchbuilt locomotive is a North British Railway 0–6–0. Snow effects need care to be convincing. Note how the snow is "melted" in areas such as the warmer roof of the freight shed. (Model by Steve Barnfield)

Left This is the fictitious village of Moors End in the English county of Cornwall, imagined and constructed by a Dutch modeler. The entire scene occupies an area of less than 5 sq ft (1.5 sq m) and is built to 1:76 scale. Note the superb texture and detail of the structures and the well-observed trees. (Model by Reiner Hendriksen)

Above Snow scene at Red Mountain Town in Colorado, modeled in HOn3. The modeling is based on historic photos and old surveys. The snow was done with plaster. (Model by Robert Ross)

Above Materials and careful painting combine successfully in this water tower. The stonework is carved modeling clay on a foamboard base, and the tank is a simple styrene box. Time spent dry-brushing the rust effect paid off, and details such as the pipe are shown to full advantage. (Model by Christopher Payne)

Above This dramatic model portrays a masonry and wood fan trestle bridge of the type designed by the 19th-century engineer Brunel. The original was once a distinctive feature of the British Great Western Railway. It is in 1:76 scale. (Model by The Pendon Museum)

Above The Pine Point Mill logging railroad is to HO scale and was inspired by scenes in British Columbia. A Mallet locomotive slowly crosses the typical old-time trestle bridge, and the water that it spans is real, contrary to usual small scale model practise! (Model by Mike Ruby)

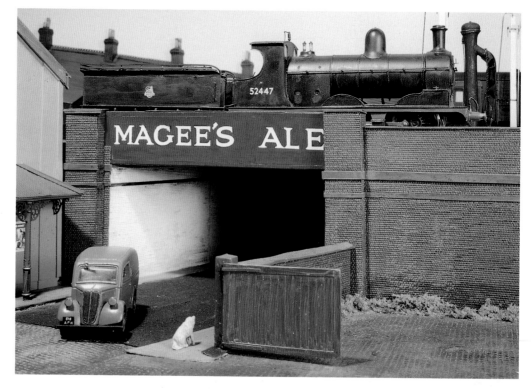

Above A typical British city scene features in this Platt Lane O gauge layout, where a plate girder bridge, carrying an advert for the local brewery, crosses a back street. (Model by Trevor Booth)

Left The lure and drama of Colorado narrow gauge railroads are captured on this freelanced HOn3 Silver San Juan Railroad. The engine house and smaller structures are all scratch-built, using northeastern wood and Grandt Line window and door castings. Details are everywhere, and add to the atmosphere of a working railroad. (Model by Ken Dzuiba)

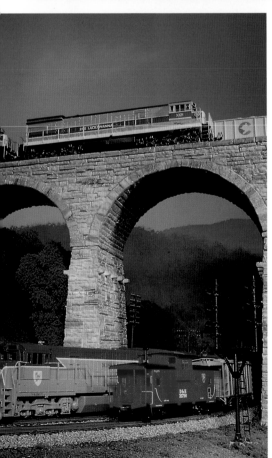

Left Some modelers go to the absolute limits in re-creating a scene that existed on an actual railroad. Harold Werthwein models the Erie Railroad and his scene of the famous Starucca Viaduct in north eastern Pennsylvania is correct right down to the trees. The locomotives are Atlas HO GE U-33 and U-36C diesels.

Above Fine modeling in 1:76 scale (4mm or 1/64in to 1 ft) results in a perfect representation of a typical stone-block viaduct of the type found in northern England. The tree modeling is also noteworthy. (Model by Shipley Model Railway Society, UK)

Left Catfish depot, jetty, and the steeply ascending main street on the Catfish Creek and Bear Mountain HO layout built by a British modeling group. This layout has won awards for its superb "backwoods" character and high degree of detailing. On the hillside above, a small diesel switcher hauls a gondola from the local mine. (Model by the Midnight Oilers)

Left Most logging railroad models include a sawmill scene, but few modelers remember to add bark and other debris in the log pond. The mountain water has an authentic "root beer" tint. This is the On3 Leaville & Denniston, a logging railroad set in California's Sierra foothills. (Model by the late Bob Love, and his son Dennis)

Left The infamous Captain Queeg is memorialized in the marine salvage company on this HO scale railroad. The floor of the harbor was detailed with seaweed from ground foam and trash, then clear resin was poured inside a form for the water. (Model by Karl Warden)

Above A scene on the Tidmeric Minerals Company layout, modeled at ⁵/₁₆in (7mm) to 1ft (British O gauge). This line, however, is narrow gauge at 14mm, depicting a real gauge of 2ft (60cm). (Model by the Twickenham and District Model Railway Club, UK)

Left In this scene on the HO Oregon Railroad and Navigation layout, a Shay-type locomotive hauls a train of empty log cars from the unloading shed on a logging line set in the northwest "backwoods." Trestle bridges and deep cuts in mountain terrain make this an exciting layout. (Model by Roy Ashby)

Left This US Marine in 2¼in (54mm) scale was assembled from a standard plastic kit and is posed on a simple base with long grass. The result is striking, achieved with minimal scenic work and good figure painting. (Model by Christopher Payne)

Above The view gains its effect from the combination of three elements — a modified mounted figure, a detailed paint finish, and a simple piece of scratchbuilding for the scenic setting. (Model by Christopher Payne)

Left "Minanomote No Kuro Yoshitsure," a Samurai, painted by Spanish modeler Jesus Gamarra. It is from a Spanish Benito Miniatures 2¼in (54mm) scale kit, and was awarded a silver medal in the 1995 Euro Militaire competition.

Left British Eighth Army infrantry, made from Airfix Multipose (variable position) plastic kits in 2¼in (54mm) scale, and depicting a typical desert war scene in North Africa in 1942. The simple diorama display base is a spare length of chipboard, covered with sand and small stones sprinkled over a layer of glue. (Models by Roy Dilley)

Above A close view of a World War I trench scene diorama with a British soldier standing in the entrance to the dugout, and wood supports, duckboards, and sandbags all fully modeled. (Model by Christopher Payne)

Above This diorama shows two Waffen-SS colleagues posing for a snapshot in front of a Tiger tank in 1944. They are converted 1:35 scale figures painted to a high standard, and the Tiger tank is from the Tamiya kit. (Model by Verlinden)

Left Motorcycles are always popular in model form and many kits are available. Typical of the most highly detailed is this 1:12 scale model of a BMW 80G/S and rider of the 1984 Paris–Dakar race from a Tamiya kit.

Right This depot foreman on a model railroad is made of plastic, and was converted from German to British-style uniform by carving with a sharp knife. The wicker hampers are commercial accessories. (Model by Christopher Payne)

Left The brewery worker, modified from a kit figure, is posed with a barrel in a freight bay. The scale is 1:34. (Model by Christopher Payne)

Left The Moroccan Wedding Party (*La Noce Marocaine*) is entirely scratchbuilt in 1:32 scale to a high degree of detail and finish. This piece won a gold award at the 1995 Euro Militaire for French modeler Jean-Pierre Duthiel.

Above A notable series of model soldier kits in 54mm scale, assembled from minutely detailed plastic components, is produced by the French company Historex, concentrating mostly on the armies of the Napoleonic Wars. This is a French Fourth Lancers figure from the Battle of Waterloo period (1815). (Model by Historex Agents)

Above This scratchbuilt Uhlan warrior was painted in oil colors. All of the detail parts, such as spear and arrows, were individually made and painted before being set in place. (Model of Ben Payne)

Left "San Romano 1432" is a 2½in (60mm) figure from a metal cast commercial kit made by J & J Models of Italy, and typifies the good detail possible with larger scale figures. (Painted by Rodrigo Hernandez Chacon)

Left The dangerous close fighting of the Vietnam War is captured in this 1:35 scale diorama, which shows an M113 of an armored cavalry headquarters company moving cautiously around the walls of a ruined temple. The vehicle and the figures are from standard Tamiya kits, extensively detailed and remodeled. (Model by Verlinden)

Above Another view of the Verlinden diorama shown above reveals how an artistic eye is needed to indicate a sense of place and period. The authenticity of the military models and the style of the wall, the extensive vegetation and the tense poses of the figures, all combine to convincing effect.

Left Military vehicle models for special purposes come in many variations. Some can be converted, and others are custom-built, such as the Matchbox 1:76 scale Priest, the Churchill with mine rollers, and the Centaur tankdozer shown here. (Model by Chris Mead)

Left An unusual 1:35 model portrays an actual soldier, SS Sturmmann Rolf Schamps of 13. (Schwere) SS-Panzer Regiment 1, who took part in the 1943 Battle of Kursk. The scratchbuilt model was copied from a photograph of Schamps leaning against a Panzer III tank, and won a gold medal for Stefan-Muller Herdemertens at the 1995 Euro Militaire.

Left Another Verlinden diorama shows excellent detail and painting work on a German 6in (15cm) Feldkanone, which is being hauled by its halftrack tractor past infantry moving along a road in 1944. Again, the models are in the popular 1:35 scale, built from kits.

Left The crew of a German Tiger II tank work on their engine in this 1:35 scale diorama set in Northwest Europe in the fall of 1944. The model is from a Tamiya kit but extensively altered, with extra detail, hatches opened, and dummy engine added. The figures were remodeled in new poses. (Model by Verlinden)

Left Another view of the Verlinden diorama above reveals the company workshop vehicle, an Opel Blitz truck, carrying the tools and maintenance equipment. This project also required extensive detailing and remodeling from a standard kit.

Left A superbly detailed and finished model of a M2A4 tank of the US Army in service in 1941. It is to 1:35 scale, and modified from the Tamiya plastic assembly kit. (Model by Joe Morgan)

Left Another Verlinden diorama portraying the heavily armed and armored German Tiger II (or King Tiger) tank. In this fall of 1944 setting, the tank is in an ambush position within the ruins of a destroyed French gas station. The complex camouflage finish was achieved with an airbrush, with some dry-brushing to obtain the highlight effect.

Above The 3ft (90cm) narrow gauge County Down Railway in Ireland was famous for its distinctive diesel railbuses. (Model by Ian Hallworth)

Above This perfectly detailed model of the German E44 electric mixed-traffic locomotive is made from an etched brass kit by the Austrian firm Wienermodell.

Left Modeling in gauge 1 (1:32 scale) allows a degree of fine detail and realistic texturing which is almost like the real thing, as portrayed in this 1960 period setting with a British Railways Class 3 (later Class 37) at Lifford Sidings, built by Jim Harris.

Above One of the most famous German steam locomotives was the Class 18 4–6–2 of Deutsche Reichsbahn, used in the 1920s and 1930s to haul express trains. The model, to 1:87 (HO) scale, is from an etched brass kit by the German firm Micro-Metakit.

Left The elegance of the locomotives of the British Great Western Railway is well portrayed by this beautiful "Castle" class 4–6–0 4091 *Dudley Castle*, made from a Malcolm Mitchell kit by Eric Harrison of Wolverhampton Model Railway Club, UK.

Left A highway bridge is an excellent way to disguise a disappearing railroad track without resorting to the often used tunnel portal. On this area of Port Richmond Railroad, set in northwest New Jersey, the line vanishes behind the scenery to a hidden staging yard. The bridge is a plastic kit. (Model by Don Spiro)

Above Attractive scenic work on the HOm Bimblebahn layout, set in Switzerland. The rugged mountain scenery, the stone-built retaining walls, and the tunnel mouths are formed from carved polystyrene blocks. (Model by Mike Polglaze)

Above G scale, with 1¾in (45mm) track gauge in this case depicting actual 3ft gauge, allows the production of very large and extensively detailed models. This dramatic Alco diesel of the White Pass and Yukon Railroad is one of a large range of North American models from the LGB company which first established this scale commercially.

Left A simple but evocative scene on the Portpyn model railroad layout. A steam locomotive pauses between shifts at the wood-built loco shed. These highly detailed, completely scratchbuilt models are to the large 1:34 scale. (Model by Christopher Payne)

Left The legendary EMD F7 "covered wagon," as operated by the ATSF (Santa Fe) Railroad, a standard Athearn HO product but with added fittings and color detail to portray the actual locomotive # 43. (Model by Chris Ellis)

Above The Rio Grande and Western Railroad has always been a popular model subject, and locomotives and stock of this famous 3ft (90cm) gauge line are made in several scales, mostly as limited-edition handcrafted brass products of high value. This scenic layout shows # 463, a 2–8–2, on a high trestle in a typical stark rocky canyon. (Model by Morgan Lewis)

Above Mainline freight activity by British Rail in the 1980s is seen on the accurately modeled Law Junction layout of Nottingham (Bulwell) Model Railway Society, UK. This 1:76 scale layout features authentic overhead pickup, and the Class 87 electric locomotives are by Lima. Note the realistic texture of the grassy bank.

Above A combination of trees and mountain terrain make Swiss railroads a popular layout theme. This HOm line is based on an imaginary branch of the famous Rhätische Bahn, and shows a Krokodil (Crocodile) locomotive of the company arriving at Weisenhang with a freight train. The track is 12mm depicting the real meter gauge. (Model by Mike Polglaze)

Above A novel idea for a layout is this World War II dockyard with a "Flower" class corvette and MTBs (FPBs) alongside the jetty. (Model by Chris Mead)

Above An evocative World War II atmosphere is captured on this layout, where a freight train has just brought stores for loading onto the naval cargo ship shown in the foreground. The ship, warehouse, and jetty details are of a very high standard. (Model by Peter Bossom)

Above This well modeled quayside scene on the German North Sea coast is on a narrow gauge layout. The fishing boat is from a Kibri 1:87 scale kit, and the Mariensel layout is to HOe 1:87 scale on 9mm gauge track. (Model by Rolf Knipper)

Above A superb model in 1:32 scale (matching gauge 1 model railroads) – about 2ft (60cm) long. Scratchbuilt in wood, metal, and plastic, it depicts a typical Clyde Puffer (cargo coaster) of the 1930s in faithful detail. The flat bottom enabled the boat to dry out for unloading over the beach during low tide. (Model by B.E. Clark)

Left Another view from the Mariensel HOe layout of Rolf Knipper, which depicts a German North Sea fishing port served by narrow gauge railroad. This picture is not much smaller than the actual size of the model, illustrating its precision. The jetty piling and frontage are particularly notable.

Left Effective water modeling on an HO Oregon Railroad and Navigation layout. The "wet" look was achieved by repeated coats of clear gloss varnish, applied over a plaster base painted with blacks, browns, and dark greens. Note also the realistic "backwoods" atmosphere, typical of the northwest logging lines of old. (Model by Roy Ashby)

Left A fine example of scratchbuilt modeling. This superb 1:48 scale model of the British Admiralty tug *Confiance* is made of wood, metal, and plastic, and is powered by an electric motor with radio control for realistic maneuvering. It is pictured underway in a swimming pool.

Above Although it is as smooth as glass, this water is poured plastic resin. The scene in HO scale, represents a fishing company's wharf and packing plant on Florida's Gulf Coast. The rockwork is hand-carved. Nearly everything in the scene, including the boats and many of the fittings on them, are scratchbuilt. (Model by Ron Dillon)

Above An interesting variation by a kit maker alters a standard tractor unit into a wrecker truck, a conversion often seen in real life. Extensive additions are needed to provide the boom, winch, and rear platform and come as extra parts in the kit. This is modeled from a 1:25 scale AMT kit. (Model by Ted Taylor)

Above This DAF 2800 was modeled from an Italeri 1:25 kit, with added detail and an impeccable finish. Note the front lock on the wheels, an alteration which gives added authenticity: many models are constructed with the front wheels rigidly straight, whereas real vehicles are more often seen with some wheel lock applied. (Model by Ted Taylor)

Left Another view of the wrecker model above, which is based on a Peterbilt conventional tractor. Thread was used to make the winch cable, and a strengthened front bumper and warning beacons were included with the kit. (Model by Ted Taylor)

Right A scene on an HO scale CSX railroad along the eastern seaboard of the U.S. with hundreds of vehicles and countless scale realistically posed figures. Notice the combination of old and new: the brick gas station is typical of the 1940s–1950s, while the thru-way truckstop copies today's convenience store/gas station. (Model by Michael Nixon)

Left This 1:25 scale Mack "R" series conventional tractor has been made straight from the kit and left in gleaming "show" condition, so that its rugged lines and standard detail can be appreciated. (Model by Ted Taylor)

Above Fire engines make colorful and dramatic models. This La France pumper is in the colors and markings of the Baltimore Fire Department, and is made in 1:25 scale from a kit. (Model by Ted Taylor)

Left Complementing the pumper is the ladder company vehicle, another La France unit, built from a kit that uses the same chassis and cab parts. This 1:25 scale model is in the scheme of the Elmira Fire Department. (Model by Ted Taylor)

Above This 1:25 scale Kenworth in high visibility finish and
fairings depicts the transporter vehicle for the Super Boss truck
dragster. (Model by Ted Taylor)

Left In a model collection, contrasts can
be interesting. This Kenworth tractor with
sleeper cab is basically the same unit as
shown above in modified form, but without
the shrouding and extra equipment
associated with competitions, and
portraying the everyday working
appearance of a typical American rig.
(Model by Ted Taylor)

Left An example of a perfectly detailed White Freightliner 6 x 4 built from an AMT kit in 1:25 scale. Every possible external fitting is added, including the airbrake pipes and the mass of license plates for interstate operation. (Model by Ted Taylor)

Left A 1:24 scale Australian Mack Truck Road train model. The tractor unit is by Italeri and the trailer is by Revell. The trailer is made straight from the kit, with added mudflaps made from plastic card. The tractor unit is modified with massive long-range fuel tanks, windshield stoneguard, and an air tank for the starter motor. (Model by Ted Taylor)

Above Two views of a 1:25 scale Scania LB 141 tractor unit from a Heller kit. Many details were added, including airbrake pipes and supports, spare-wheel carrier, chassis tray, and the run-up ramps on the chassis rear. The cab door was made to open using hinges made from thick plastic card strip. (Model by Ted Taylor)

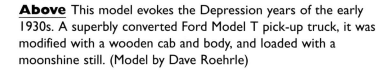

Above This model evokes the Depression years of the early 1930s. A superbly converted Ford Model T pick-up truck, it was modified with a wooden cab and body, and loaded with a moonshine still. (Model by Dave Roehrle)

Right This 1:48 scale F-4G Wild Weasel Phantom II *City of Victorville* operated out of George AFB and was in service from the Vietnam War until 1996. Wild Weasels were used to detect and destroy enemy missile sites. This model is made straight from a Hasegawa kit, and has an airbrush finish with over 180 supplied decals. (Model by Ted Taylor)

Left This US Navy F–14A Tomcat is displayed on a diorama base made from a printed series on thin cardboard. This gives a realistic depiction of a portion of an aircraft carrier deck. It is mounted, in turn, on a plywood base. The tractors and maintenance equipment are from accessory sets. The scale is 1:72. (Model by Verlinden)

Right A 1:32 scale Matchbox/Revell Aerospatiale Puma. The kit is well detailed with full interior fittings and moving panels. Camouflage was airbrushed to get accurate soft edges as on the actual paint scheme. Fine nylon thread was added for the aerials. (Model by Ted Taylor)

Left Another model built straight from the kit is this 1:72 scale Fairchild C–119G Packet, or Flying Boxcar. It was finished with an airbrush in authentic Italian Air Force colors. Care was needed in decal application to get perfectly straight walkway lines. (Model by Ted Taylor)

Left This Boeing KC–135A Stratotanker is made from an AMT/ERTL kit and is complete with all of the details provided, including the "flying boom" air refueling probe under the tail. The model is finished in ADC gray and uses the decals from the kit. (Model by Ted Taylor)

Right Grumman Avenger of the US Navy, 1944 Pacific Theater, modeled from a Monogram 1:48 scale kit. The model was posed against a Pacific Island travel poster. (Model by L. Boven)

Left This DC–130 Hercules Drone Carrier is made from a 1:72 scale Italeri kit, although a 1:48 scale version is also available. The Drone Carrier is used for launching unpiloted fast targets for jet fighter shooting practice. The model is built straight from the kit but needed careful masking and painting for a high-quality finish. (Model by Ted Taylor)

Left This superbly detailed and finished Fleet Air Arm Fairey Firefly AS5 was modeled from a PP Aeroparts vac-form kit in 1:48 scale. Note the sharply masked demarcation lines between the colors and the carefully applied decals. (Model by Ted

Right A 1:32 scale F-4E Phantom II of the Vietnam War period, built from a 1977 Revell kit. This required much additional detail, including canopy hinges, reshaped undercarriage doors, reshaped intakes, cockpit fittings, and fuse extenders on the bombs. (Model by Ted Taylor)

Presentation

Some modelmakers derive all of their enjoyment from the challenges faced during the process of design and construc-tion. Most of us, however, want to see and show the result of our work, especially if we feel that our model captures something special – and perhaps unique.

Because models are miniatures, the uninitiated are sometimes inclined to regard them as toys and to underestimate the amount of skill and dedication involved in making them. In fact, modelmaking that goes beyond assembling a commer-cial kit exactly according to the instructions is similar to painting, sculpture, and even theater. Model-making is an art form – and sometimes a very complex and sophisticated one.

Why does a modeler, or any artist, choose a particular subject for a work? Perhaps to record a historical event, or a moment of heroism, as a homage to the mechanical achieve-ments of a past age, or to evoke the atmosphere of a time, place, and way of life long vanished. Two modelers might select the same subject for different reasons. Their respective creations may be equally attractive

and yet dissimilar: the distinction will arise from their individual perception, and demonstrate the varied ways of imbuing a model with charm and power. Among the many thousands of models shown in exhibitions, some will haunt the memory decades later because of their originality and audacity. These are the influences that can stimulate new ideas.

The presentation of models is therefore important for the pleasure of the viewer as well as the builder. The modelmaker becomes the presenter of a tableau, and possibly – in the case of a model railroad, for example – a performing artist. That presentation needs planning for the models to be appreciated and enjoyed as they deserve. Think about the work of a play-wright: the lines read without conviction will be lifeless, yet delivered with skill they can be compelling. The same is true when displaying a model.

The edge of reality

Whatever the size of a model – whether it is a single figure on a small base, or a diorama of many square feet – it is surrounded by a line beyond which the world

Above The simplest way to display a model figurine, such as this warrior, is on a small varnished wood plinth.

changes. This is the boundary between the real world and the inner world of the imagination where the modelmaker's creativity rules.

This "edge of reality" needs care-ful treatment if it is not to destroy the illusion built up by the model. That does not mean that it must be blurred or very discreet. True, it must be subtle, but it must also be clear. It should be delineated in such a way that the viewer's eye and brain accept the presence of a different world on the other side of the line. It is like the edge of the stage in the theater, or the frame of a painting:

Left Model railroad dioramas are especially suitable for presentation within a wooden frame, which enhances the pictorial effect.

the distinction between the created and the real world should be so obvious that the viewer does not question the presence of the line, and subconsciously crosses it into the model world.

Treating the base

If the edge of reality is left as a frayed piece of wood or other material, it tends to be too noticeable. It is better to give it a smooth finish, and to paint it in a suitable color. Modelers use various colors, such as dark browns that harmonize with the tone of a landscape, or the shades that the prototype railroad company utilizes as part of its corporate image. Dark gray is popular because it is neutral, and dark wood stains evoke cabinet-made furniture. There is, however, one color that always works well. Henry Ford had something when he proposed "any color you like as long as it's black!"

Regular black latex paint is ideal for edges. It is easy to obtain, economical, dries quickly, has excellent covering capacity, and is matte-textured. Although it is not especially hard-wearing, it can easily be repainted when necessary, or you can protect it with a coat of matte polyurethane varnish. Black is effective in unifying materials, because surface variations that would cast shadows if painted in other colors are quickly lost to the eye.

Treat the edge of a base on which your model sits by sanding it smooth, filling it if necessary with spackle compound, sanding again, and painting it black. There should then be a black edge that immediately abuts the modeled rock, ground, vegetation, or whatever, with no gap between them. The eye will recognize this black line as the edge of reality, and subconsciously instruct the brain to focus on what lies on the other side of it.

A three-dimensional view

The edge of reality should not, however, be thought of as existing in only two dimensions. The surface of the stage may be flat, but the actors and props that appear on it are three-dimensional. In the traditional theater the performance is framed by the proscenium arch, and the audience views the scene from one angle. "Theatre in the round," however, enables viewing from all sides. Can the same approach be used to advantage for a model?

This depends upon the size and nature of the work. Single figures – especially in a scale of 1:35 or larger – can look very fine seen from all angles, and are often displayed under a glass or clear plastic dome.

However, this approach works less well for more elaborate displays. Imagine viewing a model railroad, looking across the tracks with their wonderfully detailed locomotives, cars, buildings, and topography – only to be confronted with another full-sized human being gazing back at you. Whatever the quality of the modeling, the magic will have been destroyed. What you need to see is an appropriate view of the distance. Like the backdrop at the rear of the traditional stage, it will contain the eye and convince the brain that the scene is believable.

For the diorama, and for the railroad layout that is small enough to be portable (complete or in sections), presentation in a boxed, "staged" style is effective and has a number of benefits. The first is that

Above This World War I trench scene is made as a complete segment, resembling a cross-section through the redoubt, so that the important area – below the parapet – can be fully shown.

Left Some modelers enjoy collecting tinplate/toy train ranges and displaying them on 'toy' layouts. This is the Lionel O gauge Pennsylvania GG-1 "Black Jack" electric locomotive.

the builder can determine the viewing angle. This means that you can compose your scene knowing that the viewer will always be looking at the same aspects of the model: the foreground can be designed to direct the eye toward the main element, and the background can complement it. Sometimes foreground features, such as buildings, can be deliberately positioned to break the scene into a series of tableaux. Where there is movement – on a model railroad, for example – the train's progress can be made much more interesting if it disappears momentarily behind and between parts of the setting. This increases the sense of reality by emphasizing perspective and thus persuading the mind to see the model as convincingly three-dimensional. A boxed presentation also enables you to choose the height at which your scene is presented. In general, the nearer it is to eye level, the more realistic it will seem. This is because we normally view our surroundings from within or from one side, rather than from above as if hovering in a helicopter.

Lighting your model

It is important to light your model so that the work can be seen – and seen to advantage. But it is also essential to light the subject so that it appears realistic. It is surprising how often this aspect is overlooked in exhibitions. Sometimes models are unlit and therefore hardly visible, and sometimes they are incorrectly lit. The commonest mistake is to use spotlights, either poised in clusters over the center of a scene and pointing in various directions, or bolted to uprights at each end of the display and directed into the middle. The result can be blinding for the spectator, and usually conveys an effect of unreality because of the shadows that are cast in a variety of directions simultaneously.

There are several solutions to this problem, including the use of fluorescent tubes and low-voltage quartz halogen systems. The halogen lighting is good and has the particular advantage of running cold, but it is relatively costly, requiring specialist bulbs and transformer. The standard tungsten bulb, however, is not expensive. Fitted above the front

Left Creative lighting effects can be used in model work. This night scene of deliveries being made on the Leaville and Denniston Railroad layout is lit entirely with miniature bulbs.

(the viewing side) of a model, behind the "proscenium arch," it can be very effective, showing the scene as it would be for most of the day, with the sun behind the viewer. The result – especially when viewed in a room where the level of ambient lighting is low – is to make the model stand out just as the stage does in a darkened theater.

Some modelers believe that tungsten bulbs do not permit the accurate viewing of color, but if the model was painted under the same type of light this is not a great problem. Theoretically more serious is the heat given off by the bulb. This can be solved by providing a simple reflector (of both heat and light) above the bulb, made of a piece of cooking foil, and by ensuring that no part of the model (especially if built of plastic) is too close. The most suitable dimension can be found by experimentation; it will depend upon the spacing and wattage of the bulbs. As a general rule, bulbs of no more than 60 watts at around 24in (60cm) intervals are adequate.

Secondary information

When presenting a model, you need to provide additional information about it, which is bound to be of interest to the viewer. This might refer to the subject, scale, sources of research, and building techniques, as well as the name of the maker. For exhibits in the proscenium arch style, a simple display board is an elegant solution: incline it at an angle below and in front of the model. A black board, with information printed in white, will be sufficiently illuminated by the light shed from within the model. The board can also have another function: made to form a folding front panel, it will protect the display from dust or damage during transportation and when not in use.

Designing a presentation box

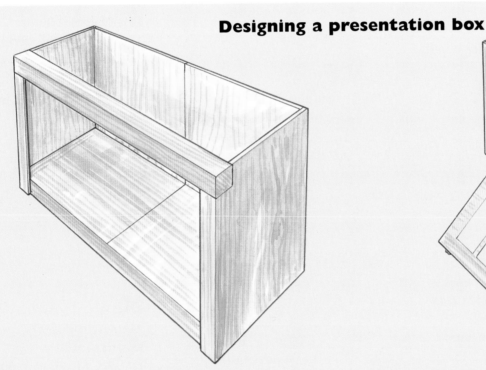

Above This is a presentation box designed for a 1:34 scale model railroad layout. The scenic section comprises two identical baseboards. These were bolted together, and four sky boards were added to the rear and ends. The end boards were fitted with side wings. The matte black lighting arch was bolted across the front to complete the proscenium presentation, and white stick-on lettering was applied, giving the railroad's name and scale. Under the arch are four tungsten bulbs: two of 60 watts in the middle, and two of 40 watts, one at each end.

Above This design is effectively a complete box bolted over a single baseboard. The inside of the folding front panel is a display board. Again, the top of the proscenium arch is the site for name and scale in white lettering on matte black. Behind it are three tungsten bulbs: one 60-watt in the middle and two 40-watt, one at each end. The box is constructed from ¼in (6mm) plywood, and the display panel is fitted with a piano hinge at the bottom and catches at the top.

Index

Numbers in italics refer to illustration captions. Checklists and captions to Project illustrations are not indexed.

Technical terms

If you are unfamiliar with any of the terms used in connection with a
particular technique, check with your supplier, who should be able to
explain or help you find the materials you need.

There may be words in the book that are unfamiliar to UK readers.
The following list gives the UK equivalent for terms that
may cause confusion.

US term	UK term	US term	UK term
Accent stripe	Chrome flash	Spur	Siding
Caliper rule	Calliper	Switch (rail)	Point
Car	Wagon; carriage	Tram (mining)	Open railway wagon for mining loads
Clothespin	Clothes peg		
Deck	Footplate	Tramroad (mining)	Tramway
Depot foreman	Station master	Triangle	Set square
Engineer	Driver	Trolley	Tram
Faucet	Tap	Truck stop	Transport café
Fender	Wing of a car; mudguard	Turbosupercharger	Turbo charger
Gas station	Petrol station	Vest	Waistcoat
Latex paint	Emulsion paint	Vise	Vice
Lumber	Timber	Wax paper	Greaseproof paper
Masonite	Hardboard	White glue	PVA adhesive
Mat board	Mounting board	X-Acto knife	Craft knife with wide
Pilot	Cowcatcher		range of interchangeable
Pilot beam	Buffer beam		handles and blades
Road names	Railway companies		

Credits
and acknowledgements

Keys to directions: *a* above, *b* below, *c* center, *l* left, *r* right.

All demonstrations and models by Christopher Payne and Ben Payne were photographed by Duncan Croucher; Chris Ellis made and photographed his own models, with the exception of page 72, photographed by Brian Monaghan; all models featured and demonstrated by Ted Taylor were photographed by Manny Cefai with the exception of those shown on pages 132 and 140*a*, which were photographed by Martin Norris.

Quarto Publishing would like to acknowledge and thank the Pendon Museum of Miniature Landscape and Transport, Long Wittenham, Abingdon, Oxfordshire, England, for kindly allowing us to photograph some of their models, shown on pages 14*a*, 31*c*, 46*a*, 101*ar*, 147*ar*, *bl* & *br*, 149*a*, 152*ar*, and 184*b*. All photographs by Duncan Croucher.

We are indebted to the following publications and organizations, who have very kindly given Quarto permission to reproduce copyright material:

British Railway Modelling and **International Railway Modelling** (published by Warners Group Holding plc): 142*b*, 145*b*, 149*c*, 150*b*, 152*b*,153*br*, 160*br*, 164*al*, & *b*, 165*b*, 168*b*, 169*a*, 170*al* & *r*. Photographs by Tony Wright.

Continental Modeller and **Railway Modeller** (published by Peco Publications): 30*bl* & *r*, 80*bl* & *r*, 115*bl*, 148*a*, 150*a*, 151*a*, 152*al*, 154*a*, 155*ar* & *b*, 166*b*, 169*b*, 170*b*, 172*a* & *b*. Photographs by Len Weal.

Railroad Model Craftsman (published by Carstens Publications Inc.): has published work by Chris D'Amato, Don Spiro, and Bill Schaumburg.

FineScale Modeler magazine (copyright 1995 by Kalmbach Publishing Co.): 3 & 170*bl*, 163*a*.

Historex Agents: 100*r*, 126*b*, 159*a*, *bl* & *c*.

LGB Company/Ernst Paul Lehmann: 81*al*, 142/143*al*, 167*a*.

Lunde Studios, Eureka Springs, AR: 30*ar*, 144*al*, & *ar*, 145*ar*.

Verlinden & Stok nv, publishers of the Verlinden Productions Catalogue: 100*l*, 113*a*, 114, 157*br*, 160*a* & *bl*, 161*a* & *b*, 162*a* & *b*, 163*b*, 180*b*.

Credits and acknowledgements
for chapter openers

Keys to directions: *a* above, *b* below, *c* center, *l* left, *r* right.

…Milltown and Mineral Mesa Railroad, by Bob …Creek and Bear Mountain Railroad, by the …British Midland Railway depot, by Julian …Julian Cavalier, photo by Chris D'Amato; … Berkshire, by the Pendon Museum; **31*b*** …ut, by Christopher Payne.

…ek and Bear Mountain layout, by the …Bimblebahn layout, by Mike Polglaze; …**31*ar*** The Port Richmond railroad, …**81*c*** The Silver San Juan railroad, …Don Spiro; **81*b*** Helmstetter's …e Pittsburgh Model Railroad …Museu…

Figures and a… …Tiger Tank, by Verlinden;

100*r* Samurai, painted by Jesus Gamarra, by Historex; **101*al*** 1456 BMW 880G/S with Paris-Dakar Rider, by Chris Ellis; **101*ar*** 1930s English farmyard, by the Pendon Museum; **101*c*** figures at an English railway station, modeller unknown, photo by Andy Binns; **101*b*** Australian soldiers, 1820s, ET archive.

Vehicles and machinery: 114 Vietnam War diorama, by Verlinden; **115*a*** Sterling Single in O Gauge, photo by Tony Wright; **115*bl*** The Nellie Peck on an Oregon Railroad and Navigation layout, by Ron Ashby; **115*br*** Matchbox/Revell Aerospatiale Puma kit, by Ted Taylor.

Gallery: 142/143*al* Alco Diesel of the White Pass and Yukon railroad, by the LGB company; **142*c*** Battle scene, photo by Brian Monaghan, courtesy of Chris Ellis; **142*b*** British Victorian school by Allan Downes; **143*ar*** The Erie Lackawanna layout, by Rich Hedstrom, photo by Don Spiro; **143*b*** Mack 'R' Series 600, by Ted Taylor.

Additional credits

Keys to directions: *a* above, *b* below, *c* center, *l* left, *r* right.

5 & 173b Bill Schaumburg; **6 & 158a** Chris Ellis; **7** Ted Taylor; **8, 9a & b** ET Archive; **10a & b, 11a** Bill Schaumburg; **11b** photo by Tony Wright; **12a & b** Ted Taylor and Manny Cefai; all on pages **13, 14, & 15** modelled by Christopher and Ben Payne; **24b** Chris Ellis; **26-29** models and equipment supplied by Ted Taylor, photographed by Martin Norris; **75** model and photo by Michael Andress, courtesy of Chris Ellis; **144b** Bill Schaumburg; **145al** photo by Andy Binns; **146bl** Bill Schaumburg; **146br** Chris Ellis; **148b** Bill Schaumburg; **149b** Chris D'Amato; **151br** Bill Scaumburg; **153bl** Don Spiro; **154b, 155al** Bill Schaumburg; **156ar** and **157bl** models by Ben Payne; **157a** Chris Ellis; **158br** model by Ben Payne; **159c, 164ar** Chris Ellis; **164b** Tony Wright/**Model Railways**; **165a** Chris Ellis; **165b** Tony Wright/**Model Railways Illustrated**; **166a** photo by Don Spiro; **171** photo by AJ Clark; **173a** Chris Ellis; **175a** Bill Schaumburg; **182c** Chris Ellis; **183a** model by Ted Taylor; **184a & b, 185** models by Christopher Payne; **186a** Don Spiro; **186b** model by Bob Love, photo by Bill Schaumburg.

All other photos are the copyright of Quarto Publishing.

Finally we would like to extend our thanks to the Scale Rail Model Centre, Eastbourne, East Sussex, England, and Squires Model & Craft Tools, Bognor Regis, West Sussex, England, who kindly supplied equipment and tool for use in photography.

**Structures: 30*ar* The ⅃.
Lunde; 30*br* The Catfish
Midnight Oilers; 30*bl* A ⅃
Russell; 31*a* Sears Home by
31*c* Vale of the White Horse
Depot from the Portpyn layo

Landscape: 80*l*, Catfish Cr⅃
Midnight Oilers; **80/81** The ⅃
81*al* by the LGB Company; ⅃
model and photo by Don Spiro; ⅃
Colorado, by Ken Dzuiba, photo by ⅃
C⅃ ⅃e, Western Maryland railroad, by th⅃
⅃⅃, photo by Bill Schaumburg.

⅃**imals: 100*l*** Waffen SS w⅃⅃